TEACH YOURSELF BOOKS

Beginner's GERMAN

Rosi McNab

Advisory Editor: Paul Coggle
University of Kent at Canterbury

NTC Publishing Group

The author would like to express her thanks to Hardy Schwarz, who has acted as language consultant for this title.

Long-renowned as *the* authoritative source for self-guided learning – with more than 30 million copies sold worldwide – the *Teach Yourself* series includes over 200 titles in the fields of languages, crafts, hobbies, sports, and other leisure activities.

This edition was first published in 1992 by NTC Publishing Group, 4255 West Touhy Avenue, Lincolnwood (Chicago), Illinois 60646 – 1975 U.S.A. Originally published by Hodder and Stoughton Ltd.

Printed in England by Clays Ltd, St Ives plc.

CONTENTS

— INTRODUCTION —

The guidelines given in this introduction are intended to provide some useful advice on studying alone and on how to make the most of the course.

If you have the cassette, make sure you have your cassette recorder nearby when you are working as you should use it to listen to the dialogues and the exercises. If you don't have a cassette recorder use the Pronunciation notes to help you pronounce the words properly. You should always *read the words and the dialogues aloud*. This will give you confidence to use them when called upon to do so in a real situation.

People learn in different ways: some like to learn rules, a very few find it easy to learn by heart, some like to learn by writing things down and others prefer to learn by association. Try different methods until you find which works best for you.

How the Units work

Within each unit you will find the following components:

Dialoge *Dialogues*

As you get more confident you should try covering up one side of the dialogue and see if you can still remember what to say. All the dialogues are also on the cassette. You should practise saying them with the cassette.

Schlüsselwörter *Key words*

These are words (and phrases) which will help you to understand the text. Practise saying them aloud. Try different ways to help you remember their meaning. Here are some ways you might find helpful:

- Cover up the English and see if you can remember what the words mean.
- Cover up the German and see if you can remember the German words.
- Write down the first letter of each word and see how many you can remember.
- Choose five new words or expressions and try to learn them.
- Count how many words there are and see how many you can recall.
- See if you can think of English words which sound similar e.g. **Hund** – (*hound*) *dog*;
  Blume – *bloom, flower*

Übungen *Exercises*

The various exercises provide practise in the German that you have learned in each unit. It is important to make good use of them so that you can be sure of understanding and remembering the language in one unit before you go on to the next.

The answers to the exercises are given at the back, page 206.

Höraufgaben *Listening exercises*

You will need to use the cassette recorder for these.

Symbols and abbreviations

This indicates that the cassette is needed for the following section.

This indicates dialogue.

This indicates exercises – places where you can practise speaking the language.

This indicates key words or phrases.

This indicates grammar or explanations – the nuts and bolts of the language.

This draws your attention to points to be noted and key tips to help you learn.

Aussprachetips *Pronunciation notes*

These notes will help you with the pronunciation of new words. However, don't forget also to make good use of the full **Pronunciation Guide** given at the end of this **Introduction.**

A phonetic version of the sound of words is given in square brackets for new words in the word lists in the early units.

Sprachtips *Language notes*

These are notes about the language, useful expressions and hints about when to use them.

Kulturtips *Tips on culture*

It is important to know something about the customs and way of life of the people whose language you are learning. These notes give some very basic background information relevant to the language material in the unit.

Word patterns

All languages have certain patterns and rules. This section helps you by providing models of the patterns of the language. When you have got used to one pattern you can often make lots of new expressions simply by changing a word or part of a word.

Wiederholung *Revision*

At the end of each unit (**Units 1–9** only) is a revision and consolidation section.

Note on Unit 10

Unit 10 is a reference unit on German verbs and does not work like the other units. Although it includes some exercises, there are no dialogues. It is not necessary to learn all the material in **Unit 10** at once, but it includes information to which you will need to refer as you continue with the second half of the course.

Pronunciation Guide

A few tips to help you acquire an authentic accent:

- Always say everything aloud, preferably as if you were talking to someone the other side of the room!
- Whenever possible get someone to say the dialogues with you. Listen carefully to the cassette, or if possible ask a native speaker to read some of the words for you.
- Tape record your voice and compare it with the cassette.
- Ask a native speaker to listen to your pronunciation and tell you how to improve it.
- Make a list of words that give you trouble and practise them.

And now practise saying the names of the places on the map:

Köln Bonn Berlin München Wien Zürich Düsseldorf Frankfurt Hamburg Hannover Leipzig Halle Freiburg Basel
[curl-n] [bon] [bairleen] [m*in-chen] [veen] [ts*irich] [d*isseldoorf] [frank-furt] [ham-burg] [hano-fer] [l-eye-pt-sich] [hal-uh] [fry-boorg] [bah-zel]

* ü sounds as if you were trying to say u but actually say i!

German sounds

Most English speakers have little difficulty in pronouncing the German sounds because the two languages share some of their linguistic roots and they both belong to the same family of languages.

The consonants

Most of these sounds are the same as in English spoken in the South of England. The ones which are not have asterisks:

b   as in bath   Bad

c	as in camping	Campingplatz
d	as in dark	dunkel
f	as in free	frei
g	as in garden	Garten
h	as in hard	hart
*j	as y in yes	ja
k	as in climb	klettern
l	as in last	letzt
m	as in man	Mann
n	as in night	Nacht
p	as in place	Platz
*qu	as kv in Kvetch	Qualität (quality)
r	as in red	rot
*s	as z in zone	Sohn (son)
t	as in tea	Tee
*v	as f in folk	Volkswagen
*w	as v in van	Wagen (car)
x	as in fax	Fax
y	as y in yen	Yen
*z	as ts in tsetse	Zeitung (newspaper)

The vowels

The vowels have a long and a short form.

The short form is normally used when followed by two or more consonants and the long form when followed by one consonant, or h + one consonant

The short form is given first:

a as a	in cat	Katze
	father	Vater
e as e	in bed	Bett
ay	day	Tee (tea)
i as i	in pit	mit (with)
	kilo	Kilo
o as o	in not	noch (yet)
	home	ohne (without)
u as u	in butcher	Bus
	oe in shoe	Schuh
		Guten Tag! (good day)

Special letters and sounds:

1 It is difficult to represent these sounds in English. If possible you should listen to the tape and practise them after it:

ä **ö** **ü**

¨ is called an Umlaut and is used on an **a, o** or **u.** It tells you that the vowel under it has changed its sound:
The short form is given first:

ä sounds	eh	M**ä**dchen *girl*
	ay	sp**ä**t *late*
ö sounds	uh	w**ö**chentlich *weekly*
	er	sch**ö**n *pretty*
ü sounds	i	f**ü**nf *five*
	u	B**ü**cher *books,* T**ü**r *door*

2 **ß** is ss:
Stra**ß**e *street,* Fu**ß** *foot*

3 **ch** is pronounced as ch in the Scottish word loch.
ich (I) Bu**ch** *book*

4 **au** is pronounced ow as in owl Fr**au** *Mrs*
Auf Wiedersehen! *goodbye*
äu oy as in coy Fr**äu**lein *Miss*

5 At the end of a word:

b	is pronounced p hal**b** *half*
d	is pronounced t Hun**d** *dog*
g	is pronounced k Ta**g** *day*
ig	is pronounced 'ch fert**ig** *ready*
s	is pronounced s (not z) Hau**s** *house*

6 **ei** is pronounced eye dr**ei** *three,* W**ei**n *wine*
ie ee v**ie**r *four,* B**ie**r *beer*

7 **sch** is pronounced sh as in **Sch**uh *shoe*
sp shp **sp**ät *late*
st sht **St**adt *town*

8 **e** at the end of a word is pronounced -uh:
Bitt**e** (*please*) Dank**e** (*thank you*)

1

GUTEN TAG!

Good day!

In this unit you will learn how to:

- say hello and goodbye
- greet and address someone
- ask to speak to someone
- say you don't understand
- ask if anyone speaks English

Before you start

Read the introduction to the course on p.1. This gives some useful advice on studying alone and on how to make the most of the course.

If you have the cassette, make sure you have it handy as you'll be using it when you work with the **Dialogues** and the **Aussprachetips** *pronunciation notes*. If you don't have the cassette, use the **Pronunciation Guide** on p.4 to help you with the pronunciation of new words and phrases.

Remember that studying for 20 minutes regularly is more effective than spending two hours at one session every so often. To help yourself to use this course as efficiently as possible, follow this study guide (and adapt it to suit your own learning patterns as you go along, if you wish):

1 Listen to or read the **Dialogues** once or twice (listen without the book first of all, if you have the cassette).

2 Go over each one bit by bit in conjunction with the **Schlüsselwörter** *key words*. Do the same for each set of **Schlüsselwörter** that has no accompanying dialogue.

3 Use the **Lerntips** *learning notes* to help the material in the **Schlüsselwörter** to sink in.
4 Study the **Sprachtips** *language notes* and **Word Patterns** as these give you information that you will use over and over again later.
5 Do the **Übungen** *exercises* and (in **Units 1–10**) the **Wiederholung** (revision at the end of the unit); check your answers in **Antworten** at the end of the book. Only start a new chapter when you are sure of all the material in the previous one.

Can you think of any German words that you already know, such as the words for hello and thank you? Say them aloud and then check them in the **Schlüsselwörter** below.

Guten Tag Herr Braun
Good day, Mr Brown!

Schlüsselwörter: key words

Herr **[hair]**	Mr
Frau **[fr-ow]**	Mrs
gut **[goot]**	good/well
danke **[dankuh]**	thanks
guten Tag **[gooten tahk]**	good day
Wie geht es Ihnen? **[vee gate es ee-nen]**	How are you?
Es geht mir gut **[es gate meer goot]**	I am well (lit: It goes to me well.)
auf Wiedersehen **[ow-uf veeder-say-un]**	goodbye
auch **[ow-uch)**	also

Lerntips: *learning notes*

- Read the words and expressions aloud. Concentrate on the pronunciation.
- If you have a cassette listen to the words and repeat them after the recording.
- Cover up the meanings and see how many you can remember. Listen again and think of what the words mean as you hear them.
- Cover up the German words and see if you can remember them.

Dialog: dialogue

Mrs Taylor	Herr Braun
Guten Tag, Herr Braun. [Gooten tahk hair brown]	
	Guten Tag, Mrs Taylor.
Wie geht es Ihnen? [Vee gate es ee-nen?]	
	Es geht mir gut danke, und Ihnen? [Es gate meer goot dank-uh, unt ee-nen
Auch gut, danke. [*ow-uch goot dankuh] **Auf Wiedersehen, Herr Braun!** [owf veeder-say-un]	
	Auf Wiedersehen, Frau Taylor!

- Imagine that you are Mrs Taylor. Cover up the left hand side of the dialogue. Greet Herr Braun, answer his question and complete the conversation.
- Now cover up the right hand side and practise Herr Braun's part of the conversation.

Übung 1: *exercise 1*

How do you say ...?

(*a*) good day
(*b*) also
(*c*) Mr
(*d*) goodbye
(*e*) well
(*f*) I'm well
(*g*) thank you
(*h*) how are you?
(*i*) and

Guten Tag Frau Meyer!

In the first dialogue you were talking to a man. In this dialogue you learn how to address a woman.

Schlüsselwörter

Fräulein	Miss
[froyline]	
Guten Morgen!	good morning!
[gooten more-ghen]	
Tschüs or Tschüß	'bye
[tshewss]	
Guten Abend!	good evening!
[gooten ah-bend]	
Gute Nacht!	good night!
[gootuh nacht]	
ich bin	I am
[ich bin]	
nicht so gut	not so well
[nicht so goot]	
Das tut mir leid.	I'm sorry.
[das toot meer lite]	
Sehr angenehm!	Pleased to meet you!
[zair anger-name]	(lit: very pleasant)
Ich habe Kopfschmerzen.	I have a headache.
[ich habuh kopf-schmairtsen	

Aussprachetips: *pronunciation tips*

Remember **ch** as in lo**ch**; ß = ss

Lerntips

- Practise saying the words (after the cassette if you have one).
- Cover up the English words and see if you can remember what the German words mean.
- Cover up the German words and see if you can remember them.

Kulturtips: *cultural notes*

Germans use 'Frau' when addressing a young woman of about 18 or more whether she is married or not. They tend to be formal and will usually shake hands when meeting you or saying goodbye and add your name to the greeting:

Guten Morgen Herr Braun.
Auf Wiedersehen Herr Smith.
Guten Abend, Frau Meyer.
Auf Wiedersehen, Fräulein Stamp.

As a general rule you use: **Guten Morgen** first thing in the morning, **Guten Tag** after about 10am, **Guten Abend** after 5pm and **Gute Nacht** when you are going to bed.

Dialog

Mr Smith	Frau Meyer
Guten Tag, Frau Meyer! Ich bin Martin Smith.	
	Guten Tag, Herr Smith! Sehr angenehm. Wie geht es Ihnen?
Es geht mir gut danke, und Ihnen?	
	Nicht so gut. Ich habe Kopfschmerzen.
Das tut mir leid.	

Auf Wiedersehen, Frau Meyer.

Auf Wiedersehen, Herr Smith.

Practise the same dialogue for use: (*a*) early in the morning; and (*b*) in the evening.

Übung 2

Welches Wort fehlt? *Which word is missing?*

(*a*) Es .... mir gut.
(*b*) Ich ... Martin Smith.
(*c*) Das tut ... leid.
(*d*) Auf ...., Frau Meyer.

Höraufgabe 1: *listening exercise:* Listen to these people and work out what time of day it is:

(i) early morning,
(ii) later morning,
(iii) late afternoon
(iv) night time

Now listen again and add if they are addressing (a) a man, (b) a woman or (c) a young woman.

Kulturtips

In South Germany and Austria people often say:

Grüß Gott!	*Good day!*
[grewss gott]	(*lit: greet God*)

Entschuldigen Sie, bitte: *excuse me, please*

You have learned how to greet someone you know or to whom you have been introduced. The next dialogue teaches you how to ask for someone and say you don't understand.

Schlüsselwörter

Entschuldigen Sie, bitte. **[ent-schul-di-gen zee bit-uh]**	Excuse me, please.
Sind Sie...? **[zindt zee...?]**	Are you...?
Mein Name ist ... **[mine nahm-uh ist ...]**	My name is ...
Wie bitte? **[vee bittuh?]**	Pardon?
Ich heiße ... **[ich high-suh ...]**	I am called ...
Wie heißen Sie? **[vee high-sen zee]**	What is your name?
Ich verstehe nicht. **[ich fair-shtayuh nicht]**	I don't understand.
Er ist nicht hier. **[air ist nicht here]**	He is not here.
heute **[hoy-tuh]**	today
Sprechen Sie Englisch? **[shprech-un zee ehng-lish]**	Do you speak English?
Ich verstehe ein bißchen **[ich fairshtay-uh 'ine biss-schun]**	I understand a bit.
Wann kann ich ihn sehen? **[van can ich een zay-un]**	When can I see him?
morgen **[more-gun)**	tomorrow
Vielen Dank. **[feel-un dank ...]**	Many thanks.

Aussprachetips

ei sounds **aye** **ie** sounds **ee**
v sounds **f** remember 'Volkswagen' is pronounced 'Folksvahgen'.

Lerntips

- Read the words/phrases aloud and concentrate on the pronunciation.
- Read *or listen* again and think of the meaning.
- Cover up the German words and see how many you can remember.
- How do you say: *I don't understand. Do you speak English?*

Dialog

Mr Smith	Herr Kryschinski
Entschuldigen Sie, bitte. Sind Sie Herr Schulz?	
	Nein. Mein Name ist Kryschinski.
Wie bitte?	
	Ich heiße Kryschinski. Wie heißen Sie?
Smith	
	Sehr angenehm. Herr Schulz ist heute nicht hier.
Ich verstehe nicht.	
	Herr Schulz ist nicht hier.
Sprechen Sie Englisch?	
	Ich verstehe ein bißchen. Mr Schulz is not here.
Wann kann ich ihn sehen?	
	Morgen.
Vielen Dank. Auf Wiedersehen.	
	Auf Wiedersehen, Herr Smith.

Lerntips

- Read the dialogue aloud and then cover up the different sides in turn and see how much you can remember.

Übung 3

Wie sagt man das auf deutsch? *How do you say it in German?*

(*a*) What is your name?
(*b*) I don't understand.
(*c*) I am called.
(*d*) Excuse me, please.
(*e*) tomorrow
(*f*) Herr Schulz is not here.
(*g*) goodbye
(*h*) Pardon?
(*i*) a bit

Wiederholung: *revision*

1 What greeting would you use at these times?

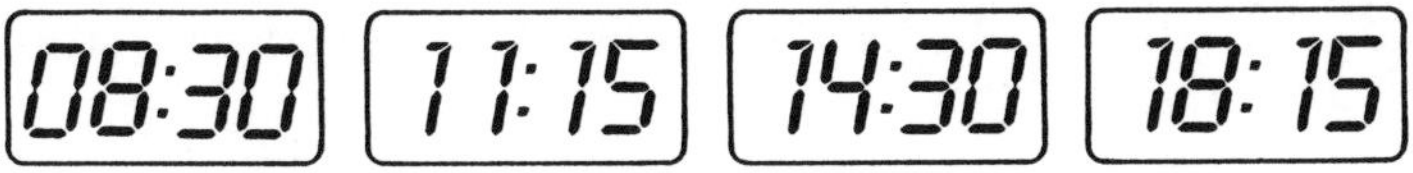

(*a*) (*b*) (*c*) (*d*)

2 Imagine you are staying in a hotel in Germany and Fräulein Hoffmann calls for you at 6.00pm. What would you say to her?

(*a*) Guten Morgen (*b*) Guten Tag (*c*) Guten Abend (*d*) Gute Nacht?

3 During the evening she says:
Es geht mir nicht gut. What would you say?

(*a*) Vielen Dank (*b*) Auf Wiedersehen (*c*) Das tut mir leid

4 How do you pronounce these words and phrases?

(i) Wie geht es Ihnen?		(ii) und	(iii) Danke
(iv) Herr	(v) Frau	(vi) auch	(vii) Auf Wiedersehen

5 Welches Wort fehlt? *Which word is missing?*

(*a*) Sind ... Herr Braun?
(*b*) Wie ......?
(*c*) Ich .... nicht.
(*d*) Ich ..... Fred.
(*e*) Wie ...... Sie?
(*f*) Er ist ..... hier.
(*g*) .... Sie, bitte.
(*h*) Ich verstehe ein ....

6 Welche Antwort paßt? *Which is the right answer?*

(*a*) Ja, ein bißchen.
(*b*) Mein Name ist ...
(*c*) Nein, ich bin ...
(*d*) Gut, danke und Ihnen?

(i) Wie heißen Sie?
(ii) Sprechen Sie Englisch?
(iii) Wie geht es Ihnen?
(iv) Sind Sie Herr Brown?

Höraufgabe 2: Check you can understand which is the right answer: (i), (ii) or (iii)?

(*a*) The speaker says (i) good morning (ii) good day (iii) good evening.

(*b*) S/he is called (i) Fräulein Schmidt (ii) Herr Schmidt (iii) Frau Schmidt
(*c*) S/he (i) speaks English (ii) speaks some English (iii) doesn't speak English.
(*d*) S/he (i) says s/he is not well (ii) says s/he is very well (iii) asks if you are well.

Schildersprache: sign language

How many of the signs can you read already?

(*a*) Damen

(*b*) Herren

(*c*) Toiletten

(*d*) 

(*e*) CAFÉ

(*f*) 

(*g*) 

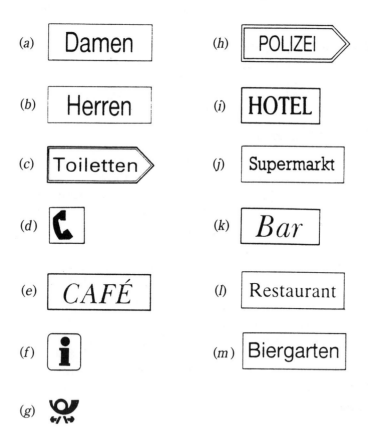

(*h*) POLIZEI

(*i*) HOTEL

(*j*) Supermarkt

(*k*) *Bar*

(*l*) Restaurant

(*m*) Biergarten

Congratulations! You have now completed the first unit.

2

TRINKEN SIE EINE TASSE KAFFEE?

Would you like a cup of coffee?

In this unit you will learn how to:

- say please and thank you
- say what you would like to drink
- ask someone what they would like to drink
- ask for a drink at a cafe
- ask for the bill

Kaffee und Kuchen: *coffee and cakes*

These boxes include the words you need for the first dialogue:

Schlüsselwörter

Trinken Sie ...?	Would you like (to drink)...?
[trink-en zee]	(lit: drink you ...?)
eine Tasse Kaffee	a cup of coffee
[eye-nuh tass-uh cafe]	
Ja, gerne.	Yes, I would like to.
[yah, gair-nuh)	(lit: yes, willingly)
mit	with
[mitt]	
ohne	without
[oh-nuh]	

Milch und Zucker **[milch unt tsook-uh]**	milk and sugar
ein Stück Kuchen **['ine shtewk coo-chen]**	a piece of cake
bitte schön **[bitt-uh shurn]**	here you are
bitte **[bitt-uh]**	please
Danke/Danke schön. **[dank-uh/dank-uh-shurn]**	Thank you.
Ich trinke keinen Kaffee. **[ich trink-uh kine-uhn café]**	I don't drink coffee

Lerntips

- Say the words aloud (after the tape), concentrating on the pronunciation.
- Cover up the English and see if you can remember what all the German words and phrases mean.
- Cover up the German and see if you can remember it.

Kulturtips 1

Saying please and thank you
If you thank someone in German they will reply **bitte,** which usually means *please* but in this case means *don't mention it*.

If someone says **danke** to you don't forget to reply **bitte**!
If someone offers you something and you say **Danke** they will take it to mean *no thank you*. If you want it say **bitte** instead. This is a mistake you are likely to make only once!

Kulturtips 2

Germans tend to drink a lot of coffee, and they drink quite strong 'real' coffee in preference to instant coffee. It is usually served with cold milk or Kaffeesahne (cream for coffee – like evaporated milk) and white sugar (Zucker) or Kandis (crystallised sugar lumps).

If you want decaffeinated coffee you ask for **coffeinfrei** [coffaynfry] ie. free of caffeine or **entcoffeinierten Kaffee** (de-caffeinated coffee). If you want artificial sweetener you ask for **Süßstoff.**

Dialog

You are visiting Herr Braun and are offered coffee and cakes after your journey.

Herr Braun	Sie (you)
	Guten Tag, Herr Braun. Wie geht es Ihnen?
Gut, danke und Ihnen?	
	Auch gut, danke.
Trinken Sie eine Tasse Kaffee?	
	Ja, gerne.
Mit Milch und Zucker?	
	Ohne Zucker.
Ein Stück Kuchen?	
	Ja, bitte.
Bitte schön.	
	Danke.
Bitte.	

Lerntips

- Read the dialogue aloud.
- Cover up your side of the conversation and see if you can say your part.
- Now imagine you are Herr Braun and cover up his part of the conversation and see if you can say it.

Wie trinken Sie Kaffee? *How do you like your coffee?*

(*a*) mit Milch
(*b*) mit Milch und Zucker
(*c*) mit Milch und ohne Zucker
(*d*) mit Zucker und ohne Milch
(*e*) Ich trinke keinen Kaffee

Ich trinke lieber Tee: *I prefer tea*

In the first dialogue of this unit you were in Germany, now Herr Braun is visiting you. What are you going to offer him?

Schlüsselwörter

Wie war die Reise? **[vee var dee rye-zuh?)**	How was the journey?
Ich bin müde. **[ich bin mew-duh]**	I am tired.
Ich trinke lieber ... **[ich trink-uh lee-buh]**	I would prefer ... (lit: I drink rather ...)
Tee **[tay]**	tea
oder **[ode-uh]**	or
Zitrone **[tsit-rone-uh]**	lemon
keinen Zucker **[kine-en tsuckuh]**	no sugar
Schokoladekuchen **[shock-o-lahd-uh-koochen]**	chocolate cake

Sprachtips: *language notes*

In German new words are often made by adding two (or more) words together. When you meet one of these long words look for the place where it divides and work out what the different parts mean eg.

Schokoladekuchen	= Schokolade	+	Kuchen
	= *chocolate*		*cake*
Biergarten	= Bier	+	Garten
	= *beer*		*garden*

Lerntips

- Say the words aloud (after the tape).
- Cover up the English and check you know what they mean.
- Now cover the German and see if you can say the German words.

Übung 1

Was trinken Sie? *What are you drinking?*

(a)

(b)

(c)

(d)

(e)

Alkoholfreie Getränke *non-alcoholic drinks*:

(f)

(g)

(h)

(i)

(j)

Dialog

Sie	Herr Braun
Hallo, Herr Braun. Wie geht es Ihnen?	
	Gut, danke und Ihnen?
Wie war die Reise?	
	Nicht so gut. Ich bin müde.
Trinken Sie eine Tasse Kaffee?	

Ich trinke lieber Tee.

Mit Milch oder mit Zitrone?

Mit Milch.

Und Zucker?

Nein. Kein' Zucker.*

Ein Stück Schokoladekuchen?

Gerne.

Bitte schön.

Danke.

Bitte.

*The correct form is **keinen Zucker** but most people miss off the **-en** when they are speaking.

Lerntips

- Practise both sides of the conversation.
- Think about what the words and phrases mean as you say them.
- Remember you must say them out loud.

Übung 2

What do these mean? Use the breakdown process explained under **Sprachtips** to work out what they are:
(*a*) Reisebüro (*b*) Reiseschecks (*c*) Reisekosten (*d*) Zitronentee

Im Café: *in the café*

Schlüsselwörter

Was darf es sein?	What can I get you?
[vas darf es zine?]	(lit: What may it be?)
Ich möchte ...	I would like ...
[ich merch-tuh]	
Haben Sie ...?	Have you ...?
[hah-bun zee]	
zu süß	too sweet
[tsoo zew-ss]	
zu trocken	too dry
[tsoo trock-en]	
halbtrocken	medium
[halp-trock-en]	(lit: half-dry)
ein Glas Wein	a glass of wine
['ine glass vine]	
zwei Glas Wein	two glasses of wine
[tsv-eye g-lass vine]	
ein Glas Bier	a glass of beer
['ine g-lass beer]	
zahlen	bill
[tsah-len]	(lit: to pay)
rot/weiß	red/white
[rote/vice]	
Das macht 10 (zehn) Mark.	That is 10 marks.
[das macht tsane mark]	(lit: That makes 10 marks)
Ich trinke keinen Alkohol.	I don't drink alcohol.

Kulturtips

Most German wine is white wine.

The best known are probably the Rhine wines (Rheinwein) such as:
Liebfraumilch – sold in a brown bottle;
Moselwein – from the vineyards on the banks of the river Moselle/or Mosel – sold in a green bottle;
Frankenwein – which comes from **Franken** or Franconia (a region in Northern Bavaria) – sold in a green bottle shaped like a bulb.

Terms of reference:
Tafelwein – is table wine.
Qualitätswein – is a quality wine.
Qualitätswein mit Prädikat – is a quality wine that has no added

sugar. Quality wines can be:

Kabinett – (the grapes are picked early and the wine is drier);
Spätlese – (the grapes are picked late and are probably sweeter);
Auslese, Beerenauslese and **Trockenbeerenauslese** – (sweeter wines)

Zum Wohl! [ts-oom vole) *Cheers!*

Dialog

Kellner (waiter)	Sie (you)
Was darf es sein?	
	Ich möchte ein Glas Wein, ein Glas Bier und eine Tasse Kaffee.
Rotwein oder Weißwein?	
	Weißwein.
Süß oder trocken?	
	Halbtrocken.
Bitte schön.	
	Danke.
Bitte.	
	Zahlen, bitte!
Das macht 10 (zehn) Mark.	

Lerntips

- Read both parts of the dialogue aloud
- Cover up the right hand side and practise ordering drinks.

Übung 3

What would you say if you wanted to order the following?

(*a*)

(*b*)

(*c*)

(*d*)

(*e*)

(*f*)

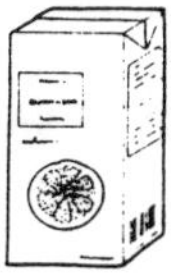

(*g*)

Kulturtips

German currency is the Deutschmark (**Deutsche Mark** in German). There are 100 Pfennig in a Mark. 2.50 DM means 2 Marks and 50 pfennigs. This is said as: Zwei Mark fünfzig.

There is more on this in the next unit.

Wiederholung

1 Imagine Herr Braun has come to see you. How would you ask him:

(*a*) what the journey was like?
(*b*) if he would like something to drink?
(*c*) if he would like milk and sugar in his coffee?
(*d*) if he would like a piece of cake or biscuit?

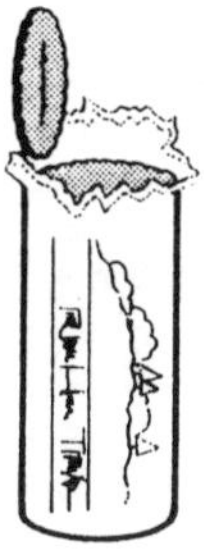

2 Now you are visiting Herr und Frau Braun in Germany. Pair up the following questions and answers.

(*a*) Gerne.
(*b*) Ja, bitte.
(*c*) Weißwein.
(*d*) Gut, danke.
(*e*) Halbtrocken.

(i) Wie geht es Ihnen?
(ii) Trinken Sie ein Glas Wein?
(iii) Rotwein oder Weißwein?
(iv) Süß oder trocken?
(v) Noch ein Glas? ...!

Höraufgabe 3: What have they ordered?

(*a*) The man orders a glass of (i) red wine (ii) white wine (iii) beer.
(*b*) The woman orders a cup of (i) tea (ii) coffee (iii) hot chocolate.
(*c*) The boy orders a glass of (i) coke (ii) lemonade (iii) milk.
(*d*) The girl orders a glass of (i) orange (ii) tomato (iii) apple juice.

Höraufgabe 4: Which is the right answer?

(*a*) The speaker says (i) good morning (ii) good day (iii) good evening.
(*b*) She offers you (i) tea (ii) coffee (iii) wine.
(*c*) She offers you (i) a biscuit (ii) a piece of lemon cake (iii) a piece of chocolate cake.

Schildersprache

1 What drinks can you get here?

Heiße Getränke Kalte Getränke			
Tasse Kaffee	2,80	Tasse Schokolade	2,80
Kännchen Kaffee	4,50	Tasse Schlagobers	3,00
Tasse Kaffee koffeinfrei	2,80	Kännchen Tee	3,50
Kännchen Kaffee koffeinfrei	4,50	Kännchen Tee mit Rum	6,50
Tasse ½ Schoc + ½ Kaffee	2,80	Glas Kamillentee	2,50
Kännchen ½ Schoc + ½ Kaffee	4,50	Glas Pfefferminztee	2,50

Imbiß *snack* **Kännchen** *pot*

2 How would you order these for your friends?

And what would you order for yourself?

3

WAS KOSTET ES?

What does it cost?

In this unit you will learn:

- how to say the numbers to 100
- how to understand German numbers when you hear them
- about German money
- how to recognise German prices and telephone numbers

Die Zahlen 1–20:

the numbers 1–20

0 null
1 eins [(H)einz]
2 zwei [tsv-eye]
3 drei [dry]
4 vier [fear]
5 fünf [finf]
6 sechs [zex]
7 sieben [zeebun]
8 acht
9 neun [(an)noyn]
10 zehn [tsayn]
11 elf
12 zwölf [tsvulf]

Sprachtips

German numbers are easy to learn. You only have to learn the numbers 1–12 and then you can make up all the numbers to 20. For the 'teens' just add 'three', 'four' etc to 'ten', ie.

Thirteen is 'three+ten'	**dreizehn**
Fourteen is 'four+ten'	**vierzehn**
Fifteen is 'five+ten'	**fünfzehn**
For sixteen, **sechs** loses its last **'s'**:	**sechzehn**
For seventeen, **sieben** loses its **'en'**:	**siebzehn**
Eighteen is 'eight+ten'	**achtzehn**
Nineteen is 'nine+ten'	**neunzehn**
Twenty is	**zwanzig**

Lerntips

- Read all the numbers aloud or listen to the tape and say the numbers after it.
- Try to say the first six numbers without looking. Now try the numbers six to twelve.
- Now make up the numbers 12–20 and say them aloud. Remember that 16 and 17 need special treatment.

Wie ist Ihre Adresse?
What is your address?

Dialog

Wie ist Ihre Adresse?

Ich wohne in der Friedrichstraße 17.

Und Frau Zimmermann?

Sie wohnt in der Mozartstraße 16.

Wo wohnt Fritz Sievers?

Er wohnt in der Bonner Allee 9.

Und Helmut Grün?

Unter den Linden 14.

Und Boris Fischer?

Das weiß ich nicht.

Schlüsselwörter

ich wohne **[ich vone-uh]**	I live
er wohnt **[air vone-t]**	he lives
sie wohnt **[see vone-t)**	she lives
die Adresse **[dee adress-uh]**	the address
die Straße **[dee shtrah-suh**	the street
die Allee **[dee al-lay]**	the avenue

Lerntips

- Practise saying both sides of the dialogue.
- Now how would you tell Herr Fischer where these people live? Note that German addresses have the house number after rather than before the street name.

Silke Taraks	Beethovenstraße 18
Jörg Quecke	Lindenstraße 14
Sandra Müller	Bonner Allee 2
Christian Schulz	Auf dem Hang 7

Übung 1

What are these numbers? Write them out in full and say them aloud.

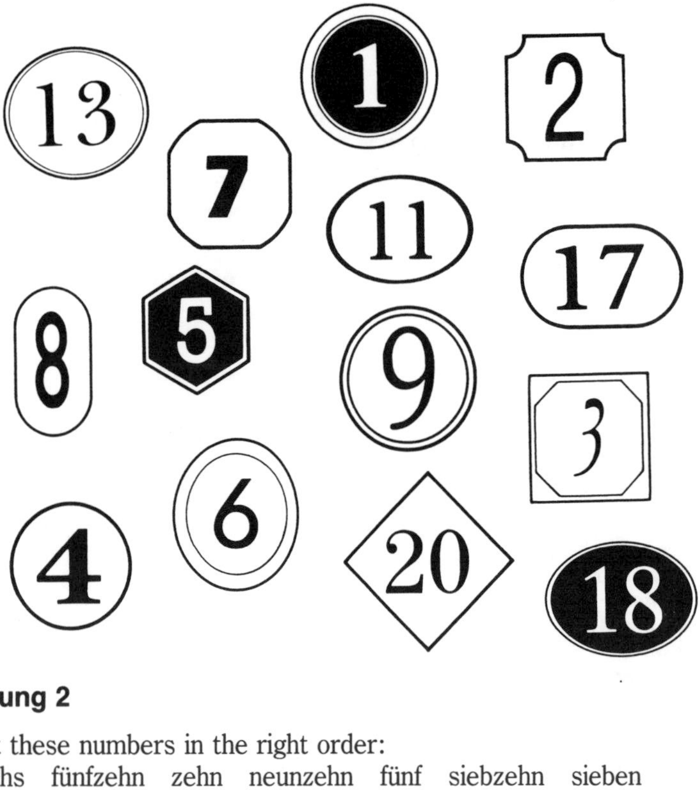

Übung 2

Put these numbers in the right order:
sechs fünfzehn zehn neunzehn fünf siebzehn sieben
vier dreizehn eins acht zwanzig elf sechzehn
zwei vierzehn neun achtzehn zwölf drei

More practice with numbers!

Schlüsselwörter

Wie viele?	How many?
[vee feel-uh]	
Wie viele Flaschen Wein?	How many bottles of wine?
Tassen Tee?	cups of tea?
Eis (ice)?	ice creams?
Stück Kuchen?	pieces of cake?
Was möchten Sie?	What would you like?
[vas murch-tun zee]	
Ich möchte ...	I would like ...
[ich murch-tuh]	
der Kellner	the waiter
[dare kell-nuh]	
Sonst noch etwas?	Anything else?
[zonst noch etvas]	
Ist das alles?	Is that all?
[ist das al-us]	

Übung 3

(*a*) Wie viele Flaschen Wein

(*b*) Wie viele Glas Bier?

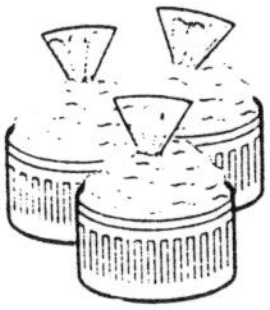

(*c*) Wie viele Eis?

(*d*) Wie viele Stück Apfelstrudel?

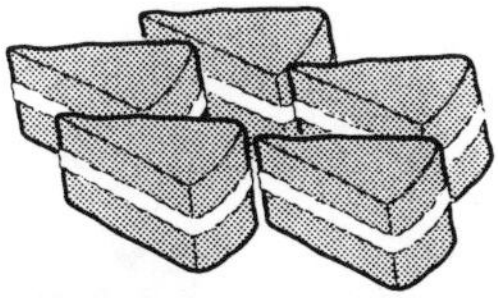

(*e*) Wie viele Stück Kuchen?

(*f*) Wie viele Tassen Tee?

Kulturtips

Apfelstrudel is a dessert made with apple, cinnamon and raisins wrapped in a thin envelope of filo or flaky pastry cooked and served with a dusting of *icing sugar* **Puderzucker.**

Ich möchte: *I would like*

Dialog

Sie	der Kellner
	Was möchten Sie?
Ich möchte vier Glas Wein.	
	Rotwein oder Weißwein?
Drei Glas Weißwein und ein Glas Rotwein.	
	Sonst noch etwas?
Zwei Glas Limonade, und zwei Tassen Kaffee.	
	Sonst noch etwas?
Ja. Acht Stück Apfelstrudel.	
	Ist das alles?
Ja, danke.	

Lerntip

- Practise your part of the dialogue.

Übung 4

Now see if you can ask for these:

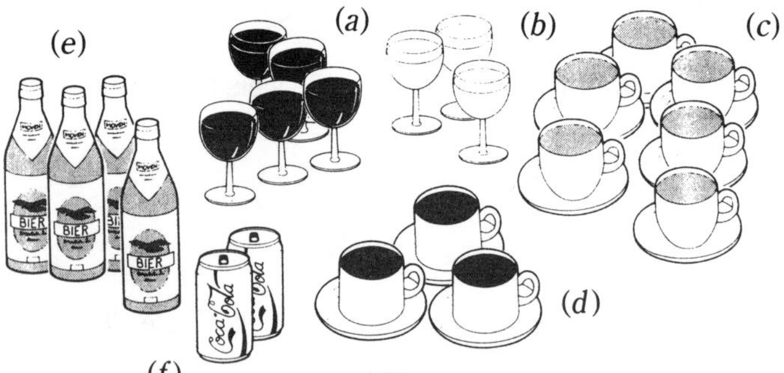

Höraufgabe 5: Schreiben Sie die Nummern auf! Listen and write down the numbers.

Die Zahlen von 20 bis 100: *the numbers from 20 to 100*

Word patterns

You have seen that German numbers 1–20 are very easy to learn. If you know the numbers to twelve and the number for twenty you can make all the other numbers. From **zwanzig** *twenty* you can see that the equivalent of the English ending *-ty* is **-zig**. To create the other 'tens', 'three', 'four', 'five' etc. are placed before **-zig.**

zwanzig	20
dreißig	30
vierzig	40
fünfzig	50
sechzig	60
siebzig	70
achtzig	80
neunzig	90
hundert	100

Note the following:

dreißig	(**ß** instead of **z**)
sechzig	(**sech(s)zig: sechs** loses its **-s**)
siebzig	(**sieb(en)zig: sieben** loses its **-en**)

Now look at the numbers from 21 to 29:

21	einundzwanzig
22	zweiundzwanzig
23	dreiundzwanzig
24	vierundzwanzig
25	fünfundzwanzig
26	sechsundzwanzig
27	siebenundzwanzig
28	achtundzwanzig
29	neunundzwanzig

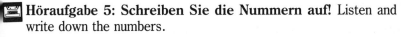

Sprachtips

When you say a two-digit number such as 21 you say the unit (or right-hand digit) first: one and twenty.

To make it easier there is a dot under the digit which you have to say first in the exercises on the next page.

To complete your knowledge of German numbers, here are the words for a hundred, a thousand and a million:

100	hundert
1 000	eintausend
1 000 000	eine Million

Was kostet das?
How much does it cost?

Dialog

Sie	Kellnerin
	Was möchten Sie?
Ich möchte zwei Glas Wein und vier Flaschen Bier.	
	Bitte schön.
Was kostet das?	
	Das macht 17.80 DM.
	Was darf es sein?
Ich möchte vier Tassen Tee und drei Tassen Kaffee.	
	Bitte schön.
Was macht das?	
	22.60 DM
	Was darf es sein?
Ich möchte zwei Stück Kuchen und fünf Tassen Kaffee.	
	Bitte schön.
Was macht das?	
	20.80 DM

Was darf es sein?	What can I get you?
[vas darf es zine]	(lit: what may it be?)
Was macht das?	How much is it?
[vas macht das]	(lit: what makes that?)

Lerntips

- Practise your parts of the dialogues.
- **Was kostet das?** Read the prices aloud.

eine Tasse Tee

eine Tasse Kaffee

ein Stück Kuchen

ein Glas Rotwein

ein Glas Bier

eine Flasche Mineralwasser

Here is some more practice to help you to get used to the sound of the numbers.

Übung 5

Look at these numbers and say them in German.
Say the digit with the dot under it *first*.
(*a*) 21̣ (*b*) 25̣ (*c*) 32̣ (*d*) 36̣ (*e*) 43̣ (*f*) 47̣ (*g*) 54̣ (*h*) 58̣
(*i*) 61̣ (*j*) 69̣ (*k*) 72̣ (*l*) 75̣ (*m*) 84̣ (*n*) 88̣ (*o*) 92̣ (*p*) 99̣

Höraufgabe 6: Now listen and write down which of the above numbers is being said. (If you haven't got a cassette try to get someone to read them to you in a different order.)

Höraufgabe 7: Put a ring round the word you hear: (If you haven't got a cassette practise saying both words and listen to the difference or try to get someone to read them to you).

(*a*)	24	42	(*f*)	67	76
(*b*)	32	23	(*g*)	93	39
(*c*)	25	52	(*h*)	29	92
(*d*)	46	64	(*i*)	48	84
(*e*)	38	83	(*j*)	62	26

Kulturtips

Germans often say their telephone numbers (apart from the code) in twos: eg. **25 42 89** would be said as **fünfundzwanzig, zweiundvierzig, neunundachtzig.**

The dialling code is called **die Vorwahl** [dee for-vahl]

The international code for England from Germany is 0044: **null, null, vier, vier.** You then drop the 0 before your own area code, eg. 0044(UK) -71(London) -7434163.

Now tell a German friend what number he/she needs to ring you from Germany.

Wiederholung

Although it is easy to say the German numbers it is not so easy to recognise them, especially when they are spoken quickly.

Höraufgabe 8: How much does it cost? Put a ring round the price you hear. (If you don't have a cassette try to get someone to say one number from each pair in German for you.)

(*a*)	2.50 DM or 5.20 DM	(*f*)	4.75 DM or 4.25 DM
(*b*)	12.80 DM or 8.20 DM	(*g*)	14.10 DM or 40.10 DM
(*c*)	16.50 DM or 60.50 DM	(*h*)	45.00 DM or 54.00 DM
(*d*)	34.60 DM or 43.60 DM	(*i*)	25.00 DM or 52.00 DM
(*e*)	50.00 DM or 15.00 DM	(*j*)	72.90 DM or 27.90 DM

1 Now try to order these:
Ich möchte ...

(*a*)

(*b*)

(*c*)

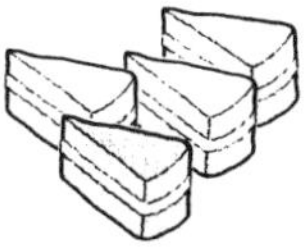

(*d*)

(*e*)

2 Read the details given about these six people. How old are they and what are their telephone numbers?

(*a*) Name: Franz Schmidt
Alter: 45
Telefon: 31 53 27

(*b*) Name: Marion Braun
Alter: 17
Telefon: 22 95 78

(*c*) Name: Elisabeth Ant
Alter: 48
Telefon: 87 46 03

(*d*) Name: Helmut Grün
Alter: 28
Telefon: 48 02 49

(*e*) Name: Silke Müller
Alter: 32
Telefon: 53 66 31

(*f*) Name: Paul Schreiber
Alter: 67
Telefon: 35 64 77

3 Can you say how much these cost?

(i) white wine 22.40 DM

(ii) red wine 18.60 DM

(iii) beer 4.20 DM

(iv) ice 3.25 DM

(v) pizza 18.70 DM

4

AN DER REZEPTION

At reception

In this unit you will learn how to:

- give your particulars when booking into an hotel
- ask for and give an address and post code
- ask for and give a telephone number
- ask for the telephone code
- say where you come from and what nationality you are
- fill in a form

Im Hotel: *in the hotel*

Schlüsselwörter

der Name **[dare nah-muh]**	the name
die Adresse **[dee add-ress-uh]**	the address
die Postleitzahl **[dee post-lite-tsahl]**	the post code
die Telefonnummer **[dee tele-fone-numm-uh]**	the telephone number
die Vorwahl **[dee for-vahl]**	the dialling code
das Zimmer **[das tsim-mer]**	the room
wählen **[vair-lun]**	to dial (lit: to choose)
besetzt **[buh-zetst]**	engaged
frei **[fry]**	free
Wie ist ...? **[vee ist]**	What is ...? (lit: how is ...?)

Sind sie ...?	Are you ...?
[zint zee]	
Wie ist Ihre Adresse?	What (lit: how) is your address?
und Ihre Telefonnummer?	and your phone number?
Haben Sie ein Zimmer frei?	Have you a room free?
die Empfangsdame	the receptionist

Lerntips

- Practise saying the new words and phrases aloud.
- Cover up the English and see if you can remember what they all mean.
- Now cover up the German and see if you can remember what it should be.

Dialog

Herr Braun	die Empfangsdame
Haben Sie ein Zimmer frei?	
	Ja. Wie heißen Sie?
Braun.	
	Und mit Vornamen, Herr Braun?
Wilfrid.	
	Und Ihre Adresse?
Dortmunder Straße 53, Stuttgart	
	Und die Postleitzahl?
7000	
	Wie bitte?
7000	
	Und die Telefonnummer?
53 14 25 74	
	Wie ist die Vorwahl für Stuttgart?
0711	
	Also, Zimmer 46. Hier ist der Schlüssel.
Vielen Dank.	
	Bitte schön.

Aussprachetips

v sounds **f** and **w** sounds **v**
ie sounds **ee** and **ei** sounds **aye**
z sounds **ts**
ß is **ss**

Lerntips

- Read the dialogue aloud and check you understand it. Take care with the pronunciation.
- Cover up the dialogue and listen to the tape. Can you understand all the numbers?
- Now cover up the left-hand side and give your own answers to the questions!

Woher kommen Sie?
Where are you from?

Schlüsselwörter

Woher kommen Sie? **[vo-hair common zee?]**	Where are you from?
Ich bin ... **[ich bin]**	I am ...
Ich komme aus ... **[ich comme-uh (h)ouse]**	I come from ...
England **[ehnglant]**	England
Engländer **[ehng-lenn-duh]**	Englishman
Engländerin **[ehng-lendur-in]**	Englishwoman
Deutschland **[doy-tsch-lant]**	Germany
Österreich **[ur-stir-righ(t)-ch**	Austria

Word patterns

In German you sometimes use different forms of a word according to whether it is a man or woman who is speaking.

For instance to say I am English, a man would say **Ich bin Engländer**, but a woman would say **Ich bin Engländerin**.

The feminine version of the words is usually made by adding – **-in** to the masculine form. Eg.

Ich bin Brite/Britin.	Ich komme aus Großbritannien.
Ich bin Engländer/-in.	Ich komme aus England.
Ich bin Schotte/Schottin	Ich komme aus Schottland.
Ich bin Waliser/-in.	Ich komme aus Wales.
Ich bin Ire/Irin.	Ich komme aus Irland.
Ich bin Australier/-in.	Ich komme aus Australien.
Ich bin Neuseeländer/-in.	Ich komme aus Neuseeland.
Ich bin Schweizer/-in.	Ich komme aus der Schweiz.
Ich bin Amerikaner/-in.	Ich komme aus Amerika.
	or aus den Vereinigten Staaten

die Vereinigten Staaten *the United States*
die Schweiz *Switzerland*

Neighbours to Germany may say:

Ich bin Pole/Polin.
Ich bin Belgier/-in.
Ich bin Österreicher/-in.
Ich bin Höllander/-in.
Ich bin Franz/oze/ösin.
Ich bin Italiener/-in.

Aussprachetips

au sounds **ow** as in **ow**(l)
ch is pronounced as in the Scottish word lo**ch**.
i in Br**i**te and Amer**i**kaner is short, as in *it,* but is long in **I**re, as in *deep.*

Europa: *Europe*

Übung 1

What is the German for:

(*a*) Germany	__________	(*i*) Austria	__________
(*b*) France	__________	(*j*) England	__________
(*c*) Italy	__________	(*k*) Scotland	__________
(*d*) Poland	__________	(*l*) Holland	__________
(*e*) Ireland	__________	(*m*) Portugal	__________
(*f*) Great Britain	__________	(*n*) Switzerland	__________
(*g*) Belgium	__________	(*o*) Wales	__________
(*h*) Spain	__________		

Höraufgabe 9: Welche Staatsangehörigkeit haben sie und woher kommen sie? *What nationality are they are where are they from?* Listen to the ten people talking about themselves and write down what they say.

Ein Formular zum Ausfüllen: *a form to fill in*

Schlüsselwörter

Vorname **[for-nahmuh)**	first name
Familienname **[familien-nahmuh]**	surname (lit: family name)
Wohnort **[vone-ort]**	home/domicile
Anschrift **[an-shrift]**	address
Staatsangehörigkeit **[shtahts-an-guh-her-ich-kite]**	nationality
Geburtsort **[geboorts-ort]**	birthplace
Geburtsdatum **[geboortsdahtum]**	date of birth
Familienstand **[familienshtant]**	family status
verheiratet **[fair-high-ratet]**	married
ledig **[lay-dich]**	unmarried
Ihren Ausweis **[ear-en ows-vice]**	your identity card

Aussprachetips

ow as in **owl**, **v** sounds **f**, and **w** sounds **v**

Lerntips

- Practise saying the new words aloud.
- Cover up the English and see if you can remember what they all mean. Look for ways of remembering new words.

Word building

Look in the list and work out what **Geburts-** means. You already know the word for *day* as in *Good day*! Now join the two words to form the word *birthday*: **Geburtstag**.

What does the word **Ort** mean? (look at **Geburtsort** and **Wohnort**).

Ortsende

You often see this sign when leaving a small town or village. It means you are leaving the 'place' and there will usually be a speed de-restriction sign beside it.

Bade- means bath or bathing; combining it with **Ort** gives us the German word for a *spa town* or *bathing resort*: **Badeort** [bah-duh-ort].

Übung 2

What do you know about Herr Fischer? Answer the questions below:

Name: Fischer Vorname: Helmut

Geburtsdatum: 22.07.45.

Anschrift: Waldstraße 34, Stuttgart

Postleitzahl: 7000 Telefonnummer: 12 34 56

Staatsangehörigkeit: Österreicher

Geburtsort: Salzburg Familienstand: ledig

Ausweis/Reisepaß: 13 72 39815

Unterschrift: (signature) H. Fischer Datum: 1992.04.03

(*a*) What is his first name?
(*b*) What is his address?
(*c*) What nationality is he?
(*d*) Is he married or single?
(*e*) How old is he?
(*f*) What is his phone number?
(*g*) Where was he born?
(*h*) What is his post code?

Höraufgabe 10: Listen and see if you can fill in this form.

Name:	Vorname:
Anschrift:	
Postleitzahl:	Telefonnummer:
Staatsangehörigkeit:	Familienstand:
Geburtsort:	Geburtsdatum:
Ausweis/Reisepaß:	

Übung 3

Jetzt sind Sie dran! *Now it's your turn.*
You are at the hotel Stern (*Star*) in Frankfurt. Practise your part of the dialogue:

(*a*) *Ask if they have a room free.*

Empfangsdame **Ja. Wie heißen Sie?**
Und mit Vornamen, ...?

(*b*) ....

Empfangsdame **Woher kommen Sie?**

(*c*) ....

Empfangsdame **Staatsangehörigkeit?**

(*d*) ....

Empfangsdame **Und Ihre Adresse?**

(*e*) ....

Empfangsdame **Und die Postleitzahl?**

(*f*) ....

Empfangsdame **Wie bitte?**

(*g*) ....

Empfangsdame **Und Ihre Telefonnummer?**

(*h*) ....

Empfangsdame **Wie ist die Vorwahl?**

(*i*) ....

Empfangsdame	**Also, Zimmer 15. Hier ist der Schlüssel.**
(*j*)	....
Empfangsdame	**Bitte schön.**

Übung 4

Wie hießen die Fragen? *What were the questions that produced these replies?*

(*a*) ....? Schneider.
(*b*) ....? Hans.
(*c*) ....? Deutsch.
(*d*) ....? Dortmund. Am Hang 35.
(*e*) ....? 4600
(*f*) ....? 23 54 63
(*g*) ....? 23 54 63
(*h*) ....? 0230

Wiederholung

Ein Formular zum Ausfüllen: *a form to fill in*

Now fill in this form with your own details:

Name:	Vorname:
Anschrift:	
Postleitzahl:	Telefonnummer:
Staatsangehörigkeit	Familienstand:
Geburtsort:	Geburtsdatum:
Ausweis/Reisepaß:	
Unterschrift: (signature)	Datum:

5

DIE UHRZEITEN

Telling the time

In this unit you will learn:

- how to tell the time in German
- how to ask what time it is
- the days of the week
- how to make arrangements to meet

Schlüsselwörter

Es ist ...

ein Uhr

acht Uhr

fünf nach eins

Es ist ...

zehn nach zwei

Viertel nach zwei

Viertel nach acht

Es ist ...

Viertel vor zwei

fünf vor zwei

zehn nach drei

Es tut mir leid. I am sorry. **Ich weiß es nicht.** I don't know (it).	

Sprachtips

It is easy to remember the word for quarter – **Viertel** – as it is based on **vier** *four*. **Viertel** is also the word for *fourth*.

In times, **nach** means *past* and **vor** means *to* (lit: *before*).

The word for 'o'clock is **Uhr** (lit: *clock*).

Lerntips

- Read the times out loud.
- Cover up the words and see if you can still say the times.
- Listen to the tape and check your pronunciation.

Dialog

Sie	Passant
Entschuldigen Sie bitte. **Wieviel Uhr ist es?**	
	Es ist vier Uhr.
Danke.	

Sie	Passant
Entschuldigen Sie, bitte. **Wieviel Uhr ist es?**	
	Es ist Viertel nach vier.
Danke.	

Sie	Passant
Entschuldigen Sie, bitte. **Wie spät ist es?**	
	Es ist Viertel vor fünf.
Danke.	

Entschuldigen Sie, bitte.	Excuse me please.
Wieviel Uhr ist es?	What time is it? (lit: how many o'clock is it?)
Wie spät ist es?	What time is it? (lit: How late is it?)
Viertel	quarter
es ist ...	it is ...
nach	after/past
vor	before/to
die Uhr **[dee Oo-er]**	the clock
kaputt	broken

Sprachtips

There are two ways to ask what time it is.
Wie spät ist es? and **Wieviel Uhr ist es?**
The answer is: **Es ist ...**

Lerntips

- Read both parts of the dialogue aloud.

Übung 1

What would you say for these times?
Es ist ...

(*a*)

(*b*)

(*c*)

(*d*)

(*e*)

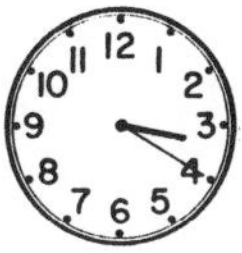

(*f*)

Halb zwei *Half past one*

halb zwei

halb drei

halb neun

Sprachtips

Look at these clocks and the words. Which is the word for *half*. How can you remember it?

Now have another look at the words under the clock showing 1.30. Are they what you would expect them to be? What is the difference? What have you discovered about the way the Germans say half past the hour?

For 2.30, instead of saying half (*past*) two they say:
half (*to*) three.

Übung 2

What would you say for these times? **Es ist ...**

(*a*)

(*b*)

(*c*)

(*d*)

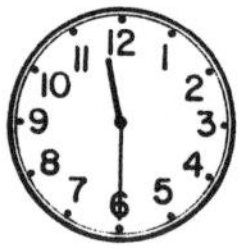

Höraufgabe 11: Which clock is it?

(*a*) (*b*) (*c*) (*d*)

Übung 3

Jetzt sind Sie dran.

(*a*) *You*	*Ask this gentleman the time.*
Passerby	**Es tut mir leid. Ich weiß es nicht. Meine Uhr ist kaputt.**
Bad luck. Try this lady:	
(*b*) *You*	*What time is it, please?*
Passerby	**Viertel nach elf.**
(*c*) *You*	*Thank her.*
Passerby	**Nichts zu danken.**

(*d*) *You*	*Say goodbye.*
Passerby	**Auf Wiedersehen.**
Now it is your turn to be asked:	
Herr X	**Entschuldigung! Wie spät ist es?**
(*e*) *You*	*Oh dear, you have left your watch in the bathroom. Say you are sorry you don't know.*

Übung 4

What would you have said if it had been these times?

8.30 8.45 10.15 14.45 18.30

Wann treffen wir uns?
When shall we meet?

Schlüsselwörter

die Wochentage	the days of the week
die Woche	the week
am ...	on ...
Montag	Monday
Dienstag	Tuesday
Mittwoch	Wednesday
Donnerstag	Thursday
Freitag	Friday
Samstag oder Sonnabend	Saturday
Sonntag	Sunday

Kulturtips

There are two German words for Saturday. **Sonnabend** (lit: Sun eve) is often used instead of **Samstag** in the North of Germany.

When making arrangements to meet or giving bus or train times Germans usually use the twenty-four hour clock. e.g. 5.00pm becomes 17.00 Uhr etc.

Wann treffen wir uns?	When shall we meet? (lit: when meet we us?)
der Morgen	the morning
der Nachmittag	the afternoon
der Abend	the evening
die Nacht	the night
Mittag	midday
Mitternacht	midnight
um	at
um acht Uhr morgens	at 8 o'clock in the morning
um acht Uhr früh	at 8am (lit: at 8 o'clock early)
um zwei Uhr nachmittags	at two in the afternoon
um sieben Uhr abends	at seven in the evening
Geht das?	Is that all right? (lit: goes that?)
Ich freue mich schon darauf.	I am looking forward to it already.
Bis dann!	Till then!

Aussprachetips

ie sounds **ee, ei** sounds **aye,**
ch as in lo**ch**, **freue** sounds **froy-uh**

Lerntip

- Practise saying the days of the week.

Übung 5

(*a*) Put these days in the right order, starting with Monday:
Samstag Donnerstag Montag Sonntag
Mittwoch Dienstag Freitag

(*b*) Put these times in the right order:

2.00h nachmittags	Mittag	9.00h früh
6.00h abends	4.00h nachmittags	19.00h
6.00h morgens	Mitternacht	

Dialog

You are staying at the Hotel Post in Hamburg and ring Herr Braun to invite him out for a meal.

Sie	Herr Braun
	Braun.
Hallo, Herr Braun. Hier ... . Ich bin im Hotel Post. Essen Sie heute abend mit uns?	
	Ja, gerne. Um wieviel Uhr?
Um acht, geht das?	
	Ja. Wann treffen wir uns?
Um halb acht in der Bar im Hotel.	
	Gut. Ich freue mich schon darauf.
Bis dann. ***Auf Wiederhören!**	
	Auf Wiederhören!

Sprachtips

***Auf Wiederhören!**
Germans say **auf Wiederhören** (*lit: till I hear you again*), instead of **auf Wiedersehen** (*lit: till I see you again*), when using the phone.

Lerntips

- Practise both parts of the dialogue.

Übung 6

What would you say to arrange to meet at these times?
(*a*) Monday 2.30 (*b*) Thursday 23.00 (*c*) Saturday 19.00
(*d*) Tuesday 10.20 (*e*) Sunday 17.45 (*f*) Wednesday 17.30
(*g*) Friday 8.45 (*h*) Tuesday midday (*i*) Thursday 18.15

Übung 7

Making a phone call. How do you say:
(*a*) Goodbye.
(*b*) Is that alright?
(*c*) Till then!
(*d*) I am looking forward to it already.

Wiederholung

1 Wieviel Uhr ist es? Es ist …

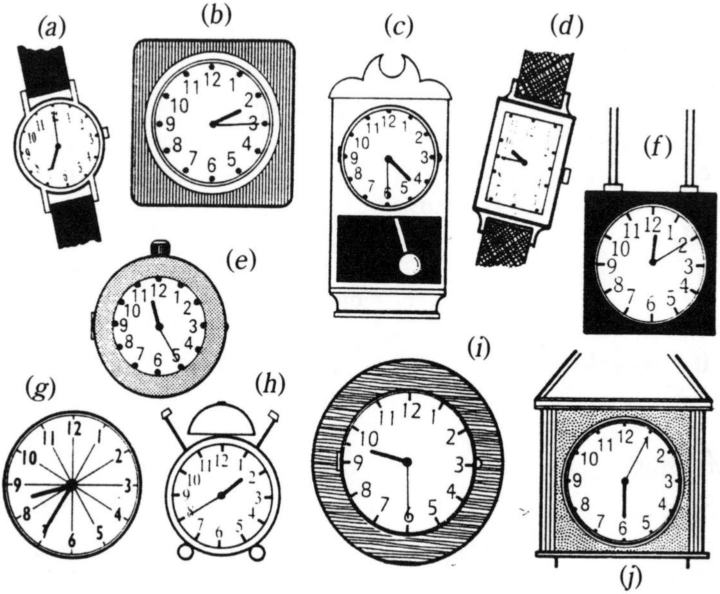

2 Und wann treffen wir uns? Wir treffen uns um …

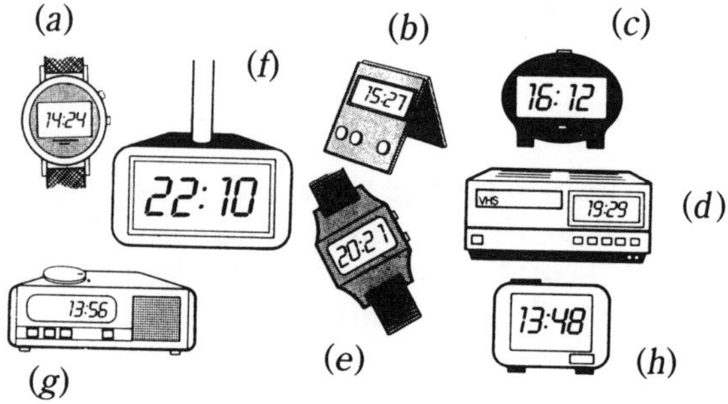

3 **Wie spät ist es?** Some of these are unusual. You don't have to be able to say them all, but you should be able to work out what they mean.

(*a*) Zwanzig nach vier
(*b*) Zehn nach zwei
(*c*) Halb zehn
(*d*) Fünf nach halb elf
(*e*) Fünf vor halb vier
(*f*) Fünf nach halb sieben
(*g*) Viertel vor neun
(*h*) Halb drei
(*i*) Dreiviertel vor vier
(*j*) Zehn vor neun

4 **Anagramme. Welcher Tag?** *Which day* is represented by each of these anagrams?

(*a*) STAGDINE (*b*) GATEFIR (*c*) MANGOT
(*d*) MAGASST (*e*) TITCHMOW (*f*) SONGANT
(*g*) SNNOGDATER

5 What times do the various timepieces show – which is which in German?

14:20
18:45

(*a*) die Kuckucksuhr (*c*) die Armbanduhr (*e*) der Wecker
(*b*) der Radiowecker (*d*) die Uhr

6 Why can't these people answer when you ask **Wie spät ist es?**

(*a*) Ich brauche eine Batterie für meine Uhr.

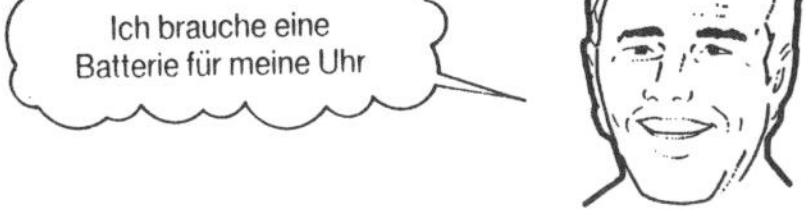
Ich brauche eine
Batterie für meine Uhr

(*b*) Ich habe meine Armbanduhr verloren.

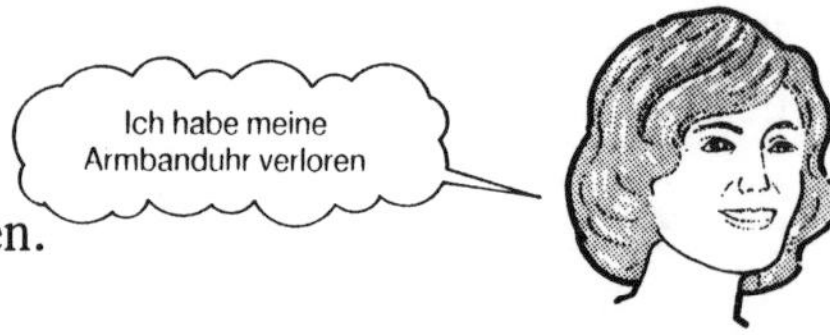

(*c*) Meine Uhr ist kaputt.

ich brauche *I need* **verloren** *lost*

7 Wann beginnt der Film *Drei Männer und ein Baby?* Read the ads and choose the correct starting times.

(*a*) 18.00 (*b*) 17.00 (*c*) 20.30 (*d*) 22.00

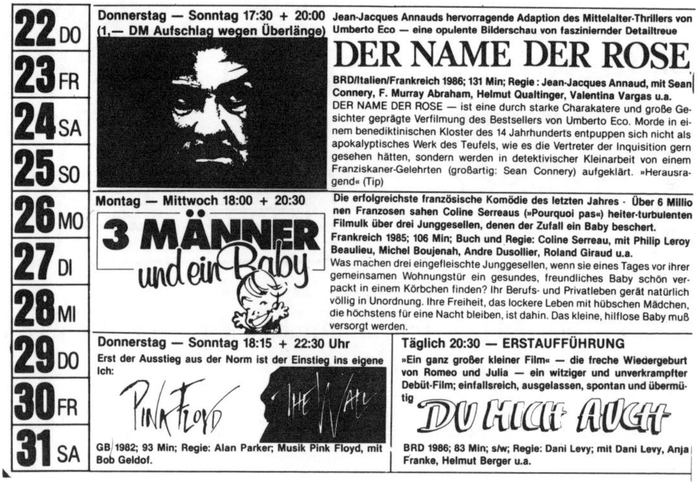

6

DER STADTPLAN

The street map

In this unit you will learn:

- the names of the important buildings in a town
- how to ask where places are
- how to say what street they are in
- ways to help you understand new words

Wo ist ...? *Where is ...?*

Schlüsselwörter

dort drüben	over there
der Bahnhof	the station
die Bibliothek	the library
die Brücke	the bridge
der Dom	the cathedral
der Flughafen	the airport
das Freibad	the open-air swimming pool
das Informationsbüro	the information office
die Jugendherberge	the youth hostel
das Kino	the cinema
die Kirche	the church
die Kneipe	the pub
das Krankenhaus	the hospital
der Marktplatz	the marketplace
das Rathaus	the town hall
das Schloß	the castle
der Schnellimbiß	the snack bar
die Straße	the street
die Hauptstraße	the main street

And these shouldn't present much difficulty:

die Bank
der Park
das Restaurant
die Post
das Hotel
das Theater

Sprachtips

There are three German words meaning *the*: **der**, **die** and **das**. Learn the **der**, **die** or **das** with each word: eg. **der Bahnhof** *the station*.

Aussprachetips

der sounds **dare**
die sounds **dee**
das sounds **das**

Lerntips

- Practise the new words.
- Check the pronunciation with the tape.
- Cover up the English and see how many you can recognise.
- Choose ten to learn today.

Dialoge

Sie	Passant
Entschuldigen Sie, bitte.	
Ist das die Bank?	
	Nein. Das ist das Rathaus.
Wo ist die Bank?	
	Die Bank ist dort drüben.
Danke	
Entschuldigung!	
Wo ist der Bahnhof?	
	Der Bahnhof? Dort drüben!
Danke.	

Entschuldigen Sie, bitte. Ist das das Hotel Post?

Nein. Das ist das Hotel Modern.

Wo ist das Hotel Post?

Es tut mir leid. Ich weiß es nicht.

Wo ist das Informationsbüro?

Dort drüben.

Vielen Dank. Auf Wiedersehen.

Nichts zu danken. Auf Wiedersehen.

Lerntip

- Read your part of the dialogue aloud.

Übung 1

A German visitor to your town asks you:

(*a*) **Ist das die Bank?** *Tell him, no it's the post office.*
(*b*) **Wo ist die Bank?** *Tell him it's over there.*
(*c*) **Danke.** *Say: don't mention it.*
(*d*) **Wo ist das Hotel Star?** *Say you are sorry, you don't know.*
(*e*) **Wo ist das Informationsbüro?** *Tell him it's over there.*
(*f*) **Vielen Dank. Auf Wiedersehen.** *Say goodbye.*

Word patterns

Gender of nouns: der, die or das? *the*

These two pages are about the structure of the language. If all you want to do is speak and understand the language at a basic level you don't need to study them. It is better to concentrate on learning the key words and useful phrases, but if you want to know more about the language and to be able to read and write it you should also try to learn something about its patterns.

A *noun* is a naming word, or a word that you can put *the* in front of in English eg. the table, the town centre, the hotel, the party, the pain, the shopping.

In German all nouns are either masculine, feminine or neuter, ie. **der**, **die** or **das** words. **Der**, **die** and **das** all mean *the*. In modern English there is only one word for *the*, but in German the word for *the* changes to match the word it is going with.

Der words are masculine words	:	der Mann – *the man*
Die words are feminine words	:	die Frau – *the woman*
Das words are neuter words	:	das Haus – *the house*

Something else you may have noticed about nouns in German is that they are all written with a capital letter.

Occasionally you can tell or guess whether the word is going to be masculine, feminine or neuter, but mostly you can't! So it's best to try to learn the **der**, **die** or **das** with new words or to try to learn words in phrases or useful expressions, rather than as single words. You will probably find some short cuts, however. For example, see what you notice in **Übung 1:** What do you notice about (most) words which end with an **'e'?** What about words which end with an **'o'?** And foreign words (eg. Café)?

If you want to say 'a' instead of 'the' you use **ein** or **eine**.

der words: **ein**
die words: **eine**
das words: **ein**

der Wagen *the car*	**ein Wagen** *a car*
die Katze *the cat*	**eine Katze** *a cat*
das Haus *the house*	**ein Haus** *a house*

Übung 2

Masculine, feminine or neuter?

Bahnhof Bank Bibliothek Brücke Café Flughafen Freibad Hotel Informationsbüro Jugendherberge Kino Kirche Kneipe Krankenhaus Marktplatz Park Post Rathaus Reisebüro Restaurant Schloß Schnellimbiß Straße

der	die	das

Übung 3

Fill in the rows, using these clues, to reveal another important building in column A.

(*a*) a bridge
(*b*) a church
(*c*) a theatre
(*d*) a bank
(*e*) a marketplace
(*f*) a pub
(*g*) a cinema
(*h*) an airport
(*i*) a station
(*j*) a town hall
(*k*) a post office

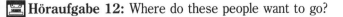

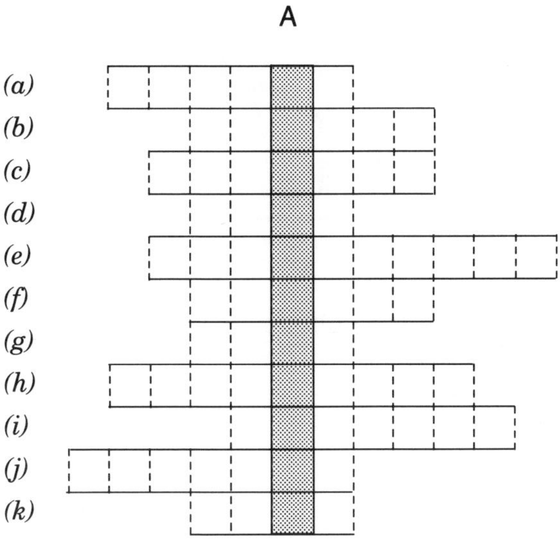

Höraufgabe 12: Where do these people want to go?

Wo ist...? *Where is...?*

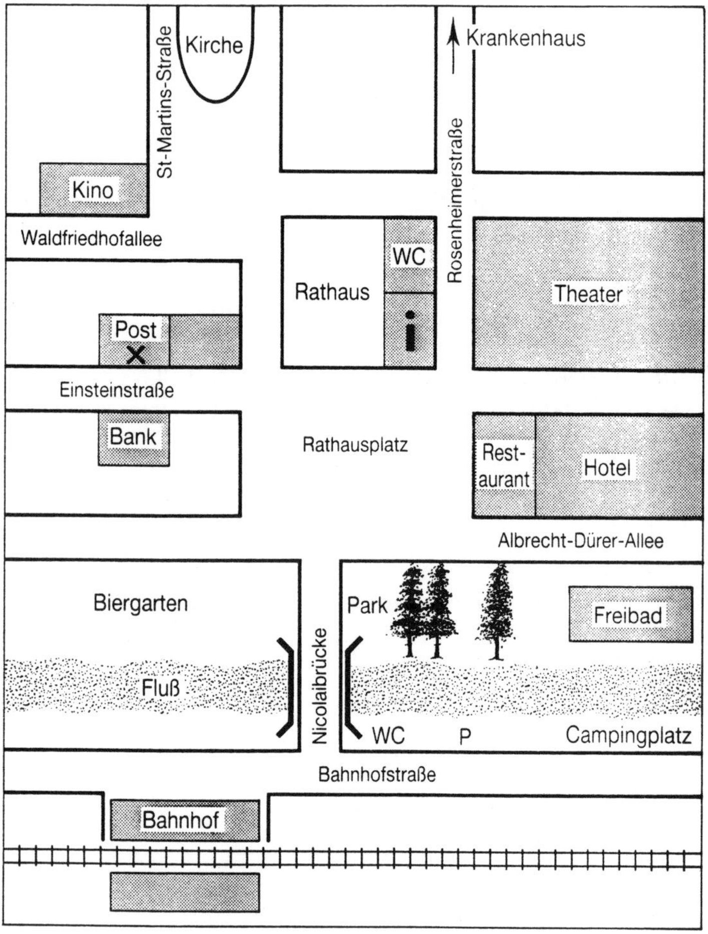

Legend ***Key***

die Kirche	die Toiletten	der Park
das Kino	das Informationsbüro	das Hotel
das Theater	der Parkplatz	das Freibad
der Bahnhof	die Post	das Krankenhaus
das Restaurant	die Bank	der Biergarten

Übung 4

Können Sie die Lücken ausfüllen? *Can you fill the gaps?*

(*a*) **Das Rathaus ist am ...... platz.**
(*b*) **Der Bahnhof ist in der ..... straße.**
(*c*) **Die Post ist in der ...... straße.**
(*d*) **Das Freibad ist in der ...... Allee.**
(*e*) **Die Bank ist in der .... straße.**
(*f*) **Das Restaurant ist am ...... platz.**
(*g*) **Das Informationsbüro und die Toiletten sind (*are*) in der .... Straße.**
(*h*) **Das Kino ist in der ...... allee.**

Übung 5

Wo ist hier ein/eine ...? *Where is there a ... (here)?*

(*a*) die Kirche
(*b*) das Theater
(*c*) das Restaurant
(*d*) das Informationsbüro
(*e*) die Post
(*f*) der Park
(*g*) das Freibad
(*h*) der Biergarten
(*i*) das Kino
(*j*) der Bahnhof
(*k*) die Toiletten
(*l*) der Parkplatz
(*m*) die Bank
(*n*) das Hotel
(*o*) das Krankenhaus
(*p*) der Campingplatz

Now give the full answer (without looking at **Übung 2** if possible), eg. Die Kirche ist in der Straße.

Word patterns

Trigger words

A trigger word is a word which **sometimes** changes the word which comes after it.

You might have noticed that the word for street is **die Straße,** but when you say *in the street* it becomes **in der Straße.** This is because the word *in* is a trigger word which sometimes changes **die** to **der.**

in + die = in der in der Hauptstraße

In also sometimes changes **der** and **das** to produce **in dem**, and this is almost always shortened to **im:**

in + der = in dem (im) im Park
in + das = in dem (im) im Hotel

It is the trigger words (or prepositions) that make people think German is a difficult language to learn.

✱ However, it is perfectly possible to speak understandable German without learning all the rules. The best thing is to learn some useful phrases by heart so that you are used to the pattern of the words and then use them as models to build phrases of your own, eg.

Ich bin im Hotel Stern in der Hauptstraße *I am at the Star Hotel in the main street.*

Then change the name of the hotel and the street as necessary.

Wiederholung

1 Pair up the English and the German words.

(*a*)	der Bahnhof	(*i*)	the bridge
(*b*)	die Bar	(*ii*)	the café
(*c*)	die Bibliothek	(*iii*)	the church
(*d*)	die Brücke	(*iv*)	the youth hostel
(*e*)	das Café	(*v*)	the restaurant
(*f*)	der Dom	(*vi*)	the pub
(*g*)	der Flughafen	(*vii*)	the library
(*h*)	das Informationsbüro	(*viii*)	the hospital
(*i*)	die Jugendherberge	(*ix*)	the cathedral
(*j*)	das Kino	(*x*)	the town hall
(*k*)	die Kirche	(*xi*)	the castle
(*l*)	die Kneipe	(*xii*)	the cinema
(*m*)	das Krankenhaus	(*xiii*)	the airport
(*n*)	der Marktplatz	(*xiv*)	the snack bar
(*o*)	das Rathaus	(*xv*)	the street
(*p*)	das Restaurant	(*xvi*)	the bar
(*q*)	das Schloß	(*xvii*)	the station
(*r*)	der Schnellimbiß	(*xviii*)	the marketplace
(*s*)	die Straße	(*xix*)	the information office

2 Work out what these words mean by breaking them up (here are a few extra clues: **Haupt** *main*, **Auskunft** *information*, **Stelle** *place*).

der Campingplatz	die Fußgängerzone
die Hauptpost	der Hauptbahnhof
das Auskunftsbüro	der Sportplatz
die Polizeiwache	der Busbahnhof
die Bushaltestelle	die Tankstelle
die Autobahnbrücke	die Landungsbrücke

Höraufgabe 13: Richtig oder falsch? *True or false?*

	R	F
(*a*) Die Kirche ist in der Griechstraße.	☐	☐
(*b*) Die Bar ist in der Neustraße.	☐	☐
(*c*) Die Post ist in der Rheinallee.	☐	☐
(*d*) Das Café ist in der Burgstraße.	☐	☐
(*e*) Die Bank ist am Marktplatz.	☐	☐
(*f*) Die Kneipe ist in der Bahnhofstraße.	☐	☐
(*g*) Die Toiletten sind am Parkplatz.	☐	☐
(*h*) Das Informationsbüro ist am Rathausplatz.	☐	☐
(*i*) Der Parkplatz ist in der Bonner Allee.	☐	☐
(*j*) Die Jugendherberge ist am Rheinweg.	☐	☐

Schildersprache

Which sign is it?

(i)

(ii)

(iii)

(iv)

(v)

(vi)

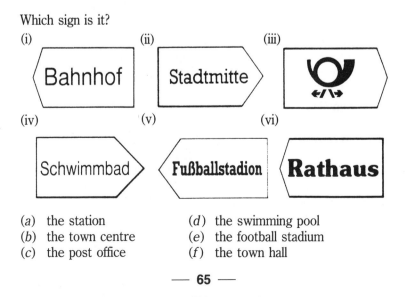

(*a*) the station
(*b*) the town centre
(*c*) the post office
(*d*) the swimming pool
(*e*) the football stadium
(*f*) the town hall

7

WIE KOMME ICH ZUR POST?

How do I get to the post office?

In this unit you will learn how to:

- ask for directions
- give directions
- ask and say how far somewhere is

Wie komme ich dorthin?

How do I get there?

Word patterns

zu is a trigger word which changes	**die** to **der**
	der to **dem**
	das to **dem**
	die (plural) to **den**
zum is an abbreviation of	**zu+dem**
zur is an abbreviation of	**zu+der**
So with der and **das** words you use	**zum** (**zum** Bahnhof)
With **die** words you use	**zur** (**zur** Post)
With plural words you use	**zu den** (**zu** den Toiletten)
Wie komme ich **zum** Bahnhof?	*How do I get to the station? (lit: how come I...)*
zur Post	*to the Post Office*
zum Rathaus	*to the Town Hall*

Memorise the phrases **zum Bahnhof** and **zur Post**, **zu den Toiletten** and use them to remind yourself of the correct forms.

Don't worry – even if you don't get them right, Germans will still be able to understand where you are asking for!

Übung 1: zum *or* zur?

How would you ask the way to these places?
(First decide whether they are der, die or das words.)

Wie komme ich zu ... (*How do I get to ...*)

(*a*) Rathaus?
(*b*) Krankenhaus?
(*c*) Hotel?
(*d*) Cafe?
(*e*) Restaurant?
(*f*) Bank?
(*g*) Freibad?
(*h*) Supermarkt (m)?
(*i*) Tankstelle?
(*j*) Campingplatz?
(*k*) Parkplatz?
(*l*) Busbahnhof?

Dialoge

Sie	Passant
Wie komme ich am besten zur Post?	
	Sie gehen hier geradeaus. Die Post ist auf der rechten Seite.
Vielen Dank. Auf Wiedersehen.	
Wie komme ich am besten zum Freibad?	
	Sie nehmen die erste Straße links. Das Freibad ist auf der linken Seite.
Vielen Dank.	

Auf Wiedersehen.

Wie komme ich am besten zum Bahnhof?

Sie nehmen die erste Straße rechts und die zweite Straße links.

Schlüsselwörter

links/rechts	left/right
geradeaus	straight ahead
die erste Straße rechts	the first street right
die zweite Straße links	the second street left
auf der linken Seite	on the left (side)
auf der rechten Seite	on the right (side)
Sie nehmen ...	you take ...
zum/zer	to the

Aussprachetips

ch as in loch **ei** as in eye **ge** as in grass

Lerntip

- Check you understand the German and then practise saying the dialogues.

Übung 2

Tell your German friend the following directions.

(*a*) straight ahead, on the right.

(*b*) first right, on the left.

(*c*) second left, on the left.

(*d*) first left, on the right.

(*e*) second right, on the right.

(*f*) straight ahead, on the left.

Im Informationsbüro

Schlüsselwörter

Gibt es ... in der Nähe?	Is there a ... near here?
Ich rufe mal an.	I'll give them a ring. (lit: I call just up)
noch	still
frei	free, available
Einzel – oder Doppelzimmer	single or double room
mit Dusche	with shower
mit Bad	with bath
zu Fuß	on foot
mit dem Auto	(with the) by car
entlang	along
die Einbahnstraße	one-way street

Entlang means *along* but instead of saying *along the street* in German you say 'the street along': **die Straße entlang.**

Aussprachetips

Nähe sounds **nay-er**.

Sprachtips

	m.	f.	n.
Gibt es	einen Parkplatz?	eine Bank?	ein Hotel?

There are two ways of saying *I go* or *I am going* in German. If you are walking you say: **ich gehe** and if you are driving or being driven you use: **ich fahre.**

Ich fahre mit dem Auto.	I am going by car.
mit dem Bus.	by bus.
mit dem Zug.	by train.
mit der Straßenbahn.	by tram.
mit der U-Bahn.	by underground.

Übung 3

How do you ask if there is … near here?

(*a*) a station
(*b*) a camp site
(*c*) a post office
(*d*) a car park
(*e*) a bank
(*f*) a pub
(*g*) a bus stop
(*h*) an hotel

Übung 4

What would you ask? You want a:

(*a*)

(*b*)
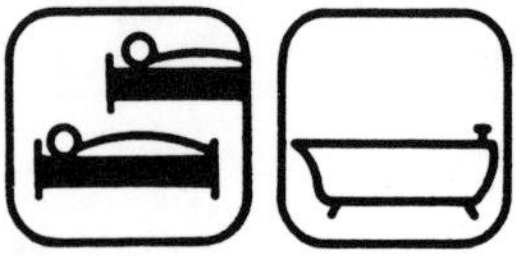

(*c*)

(*d*)
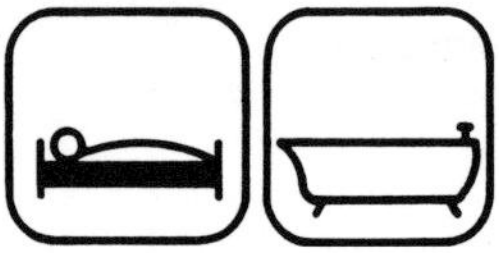

Übung 5

How do you say you are travelling:

(*a*)

(*b*)

(*c*)

(*d*)

(*e*)
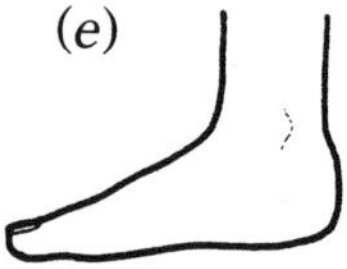

Dialog

Sie	Empfangsdame
Entschuldigen Sie bitte, Gibt es ein Hotel in der Nähe?	
	Ja. Das Hotel Post.
Haben sie noch Zimmer frei?	

Ich rufe mal an. (sie telefoniert)
Ja. Einzel – oder Doppelzimmer?

Doppelzimmer.

Ja. Mit Bad oder Dusche?

Mit Bad. Wie komme ich zum Hotel?

Zu Fuß, oder mit dem Auto?

Zu Fuß.

Sie gehen die Hauptstraße entlang, und es ist in der zweiten Straße links auf der rechten Seite.

Vielen Dank. Auf Wiedersehen.

Auf Wiedersehen.

Wie komme ich zum Bahnhof?

Zu Fuß, oder mit dem Auto?

Mit dem Auto.

Sie nehmen die zweite Straße links und die erste Straße rechts.
Die erste Straße links ist eine Einbahnstraße.

Lerntips

- Practise both parts of the dialogue.
- Now adapt the dialogue. You want a single room, and the hotel is on the first street on the right, on the left, hand side.

Übung 6

How do you ask:
(*a*) Is there a hotel near here?
(*b*) Have they still got rooms available?
(*c*) How do I get to the hotel on foot? and by car? and by bus?

Übung 7

Describe where the destination marked X is in each of these diagrams (you are standing at point A).

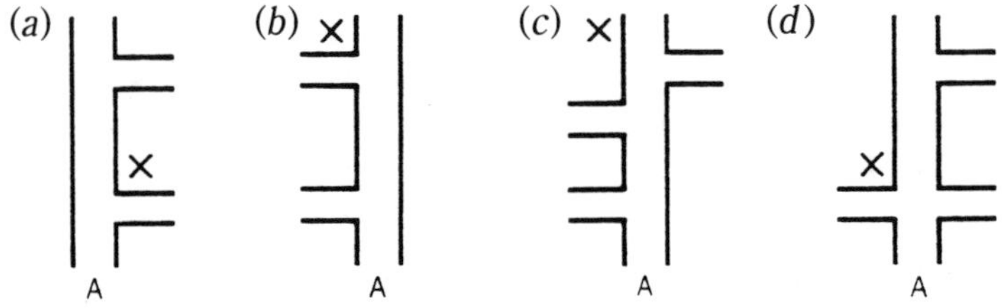

Ist es weit? *Is it far?*

Schlüsselwörter

Ist es weit?	Is it far?
dort drüben	over there
da	there
hier vorne	in front (of you)
hier hinten	behind (you)
gleich hier	right here
um die Ecke	around the corner
gegenüber	opposite (trigger word)
Wo kann ich Briefmarken kaufen?	Where can I buy stamps?
Ich weiß es nicht.	I don't know.
Ich bin hier fremd.	I am a stranger here (myself).

Aussprachetips

w sounds **v**, **d** at the end of a word sounds **t**, **ei** sounds **eye**.

Kulturtips

When asked how far away somewhere is, Germans usually reply by telling you how long it takes to get there. Z.B. (Zum Beispiel – *for example*) **Wie weit ist es zum Bahnhof? Fünf Minuten zu Fuß.** *Five minutes on foot.*

Lerntips

- Practise the new words and phrases. Say them aloud.
- Cover up the English and see how many you can understand.

- Decide which you should learn well enough to be able to use, and which you should be able to understand.
- Now cover up the German and see how many you can remember.

Übung 8

Refer again to the map on p.62.
You are standing in front of the information office. To which building do the following directions refer?

(*a*) Gleich hier um die Ecke.
(*b*) Gegenüber dem Bahnhof.
(*c*) Nehmen die erste Straße links und geradeaus.
(*d*) Auf der rechten Seite.
(*e*) Gleich hier vorne.
(*f*) Dort drüben, links.
(*g*) Gegenüber der Bank.

Dialoge

You are looking for the Frauenkirche in München. Ask this lady:

Sie	**Dame**
Entschuldigen Sie bitte. Wo ist die Frauenkirche?	
	Es tut mir leid. Ich weiß es nicht. Ich bin hier fremd.

So you decide to go into the Informationsbüro instead.

Wo ist der Dom?	
	Hier gleich vorne.
Und wo sind die Toiletten?	
	Dort drüben.
Wo ist das Hotel Garten?	
	Hier rechts, geradeaus und dann auf der rechten Seite.
Ist das weit?	
	Nein. Fünf Minuten zu Fuß.
Wo kann ich hier Briefmarken kaufen?	
	Die Post ist hier um die Ecke.

Und wo ist das Rathaus?

In der Fußgängerzone.
Da, sehen Sie, dort hinten.

Lerntips

- Read the dialogues and make sure you understand everything in them. Which phrases do you know already?
- Look at the new phrases and choose three that you think it would be useful to learn. Write them down in English and see if you can put them back into German.

Übung 9

Ask where these places are and if they are far:
(*a*) post office (*b*) station (*c*) church (*d*) bank
(*e*) cinema (*f*) hotel (*g*) supermarket

Übung 10

Now it's your turn to give directions. Use the plan below to answer the following questions in German.

(*a*) Wie komme ich zum Hotel Alpblick?
(*b*) Gibt es eine Bank hier in der Nähe?
(*c*) Wo kann ich hier Briefmarken kaufen?
(*d*) Gibt es ein Kino in der Nähe?
(*e*) Wie komme ich zum Bahnhof?
(*f*) Wo ist hier ein Restaurant?
(*g*) Wie komme ich zum Schloß?
(*h*) Ist es weit?

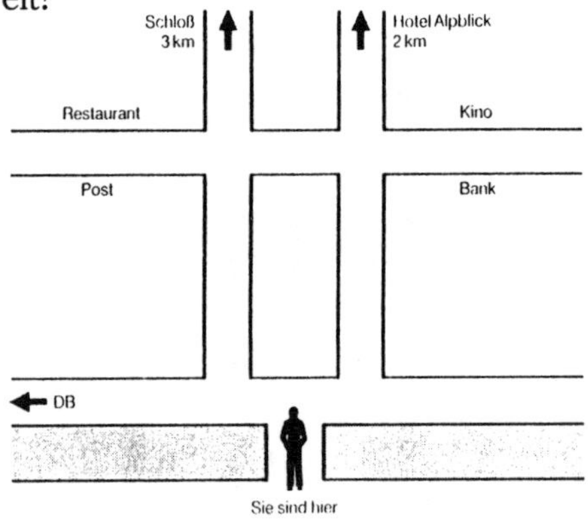

Sprachtips

In this unit you have met some more trigger words:

auf	[die Seite] **auf** der rechten Seite
mit	[das Auto] **mit** dem Auto
gegenüber	[der Bahnhof] **gegenüber** dem Bahnhof

Wiederholung

1 Can you ask the following:
(*a*) the way to the station?
(*b*) is it far?
(*c*) where you can buy stamps?
(*d*) where there is a bank?
(*e*) if there is a hotel nearby?
(*f*) if it still has rooms free?

2 Check that you can say the following:
(*a*) first on the right
(*b*) second on the left
(*c*) straight ahead
(*d*) around the corner
(*e*) on the left-hand side
(*f*) on the right-hand side
(*g*) a single room with bath
(*h*) a double room with shower
(*i*) in a car
(*j*) on foot

3 Do you remember how to say the following?
(*a*) I'm sorry.
(*b*) I don't understand.
(*c*) I don't know.
(*d*) Excuse me, please.
(*e*) Pardon?
(*f*) Thank you.

Schildersprache

What do these signs mean?

(*a*) (*b*) (*c*) (*d*) (*e*)

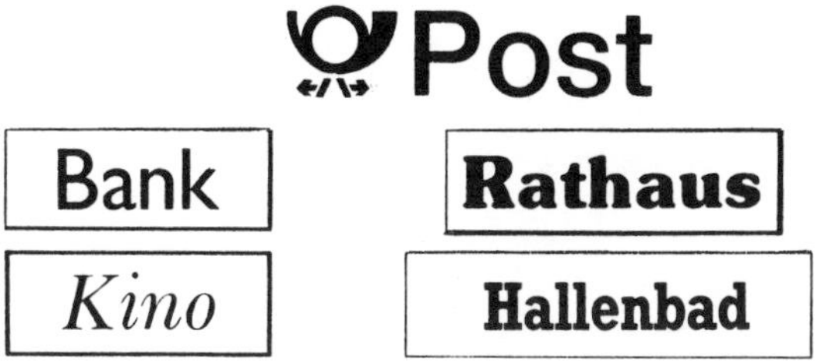

8

DER KALENDER

The calendar

In this unit you will learn:

- the months of the year
- public holidays, days and dates
- how to say when your holidays are
- how to understand an invitation
- how to invite someone to stay
- how to make arrangements

Wann kommen Sie?
When are you coming?

Schlüsselwörter

die Monate		the months
Januar	[*yan*-oo-ar]	
Februar	[*feb*-roo-ar]	
März	[*meh*-rts]	
April	[a-*pril*]	
Mai	[my]	
Juni	[*yoo*-ny]	
Juli	[*yoo*-ly]	
August	[ow-*gust*]	
September	[zep*tem*ber]	
Oktober	[ok*to*ber]	
November	[no*vem*ber]	
Dezember	[day-*tsem*ber]	
die Feiertage		public holidays
Sommerferien		summer holidays
Winterferien		winter holidays
Osterferien		Easter holidays

Aussprachetips

The italic parts of the sounds shown in brackets for the months are stressed. Remember also: **j** sounds **y (yuh), ow** as in c**ow**

Lerntips

- Read the names of the months aloud.
- Which month is it? Say aloud the full word for each of these abbreviations:

  Mai Dez Jul Feb Jun Sept
  Jan Aug Mär Okt Apr Nov
- Which holiday is it?

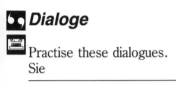

Dialoge

Practise these dialogues.

Sie	Fraülein Schneider
	Wann kommen Sie nach Deutschland?
Ich komme am 14. März.	
	Wie lange bleiben Sie?

Eine Woche.

Wann fahren Sie ab?

Am 22. März.

Wann kommen Sie nach England?

Am 15. Oktober.

Wie lange bleiben Sie?

Zwei Wochen.

Wann fahren Sie ab?

Am 1. November.

Wann kommen Sie zu uns?

Ich komme vom 4. bis zum 7. Juni, wenn das geht.

Ja. Das geht. Ich freue mich schon darauf.

Wann fahren Sie ab?	When are you leaving?
Wie lange bleiben Sie?	How long are you staying?
Sofern das geht	if that is alright.

Word patterns

Am ...: *On the ...*

am ersten *on the first*
am zweiten *on the second*
am dritten *on the third*
am fünften *on the fifth*
usw. (und so weiter) *etc. (and so on)*
am zehnten *on the tenth*
am zwanzigsten *on the twentieth*
am einundzwanzigsten *on the 21st*
am dreißigsten *on the 30th*

Vom ... bis zum ...: *From ... to ...*

vom 8. Juli bis zum 1. August *from 8th July to 1st August.*
(vom achten Juli bis zum ersten August)

an (*on*) is a trigger word and **am** is an abbreviation of **an dem.**
von (*from/of*) is a trigger word and **vom** is an abbreviation of **von dem.**

zu (*to*) is a trigger word and **zum** is an abbreviation of **zu dem.**
A trigger word is a word which may change ***der*** *to* ***dem.***
die *to* ***der.***
das *to* ***dem.***

— Eine Einladung: *an invitation* —

Schlüsselwörter

Möchten Sie uns besuchen?	Would you like to visit us? (lit: Would you like us to visit)
Ja, gerne.	Yes, I would. (lit: Yes, willingly)
Wann können Sie kommen?	When can you come?
Ich weiß es nicht.	I don't know. (lit: I know it not)
genau	exactly
nur	only
frei	free
zu Weihnachten	at/for Christmas (lit: to Christmas)
zu Ostern	at Easter
Geht das?	Is that OK? (lit: goes that?)
Ja, das geht.	Yes, that's OK. (lit: yes, that goes)
Ich freue mich schon darauf.	I'm already looking forward to it.
Vielen Dank.	Many thanks.
für die Einladung	for the invitation
Nichts zu danken.	Don't mention it.
Auf Wiederhören.	Goodbye (on the phone).

Ausspracheтips

v sounds **f**, **ö** as **ur**, **ge** as **gue** in **guest**, **ei** as **eye**, **au** as **ow** in **owl**, **freue** – **froy-uh.**

Lerntips

- Practise reading all the words and phrases aloud (repeating after the tape if you have it).
- Cover up the English and see if you can remember what all the German words and phrases mean.
- Cover up the German and see if you can remember it.
- Count how many words and phrases you know already and choose three new ones to try to learn.

Übung 1

Saying thank you. How do you say the following using the phrases below:

(*a*) thank you very much.
(*b*) thanks.
(*c*) many thanks.
(*d*) don't mention it.

(*i*)	**Danke schön.**	(*iii*)	**Danke.**
(*ii*)	**Nichts zu danken.**	(*iv*)	**Vielen Dank.**

Dialog

Sie (am Telefon)	Fräulein Hoffmann
	Hallo! Wie geht's?
Gut danke. Und Ihnen?	
	Gut. Möchten Sie uns in Deutschland besuchen?
Ja, gerne.	
	Wann können Sie kommen?
Ich weiß nicht.	
	Wann sind die Sommerferien?
Vom 15. Juli bis zum 8. August.	
	Und wann sind die Winterferien?
Vom 20. Dezember bis zum 3. Januar.	
	Wann sind die Osterferien?
Das weiß ich nicht genau.	
	Ostersonntag ist am 4. April.
Ich habe nur zwei Tage frei.	
	Kommen Sie zu Weihnachten?
Gerne. Ich habe vom 20. bis 28 Dezember frei. Geht das?	

Ja. Das geht.
Ich freue mich schon darauf.

Vielen Dank für die Einladung.

Nichts zu danken.
Auf Wiederhören.

Auf Wiederhören.

Lerntips

- Read the text carefully and make sure you understand everything.
- Practise reading it out loud. See if you can get someone to read the other part with you.
- Try to substitute the dates of your own holidays. If you don't know them use these:
  Easter: 2–7 April. Christmas: 23rd December – 3rd January.
  Summer: 14–30 July.

Wann treffen wir uns?
Making a date

Schlüsselwörter

ins	in + das = ins (in)to the
nächste Woche	next week
nächsten Montag	next Monday
morgens	in the morning
nachmittags	in the afternoon
abends	in the evening
heute	today
morgen abend	tomorrow evening
Wie wäre es mit Dienstag?	What about Tuesday? (lit: How would it be with Tuesday?)
Das geht leider nicht.	That won't do/I can't make it (lit: that goes unfortunately not).
Prima!	Great!
keine Zeit	no time

Sprachtips

Das Datum: *the date*
Dates are written like this: **den 14. Juni** *or* **14. 6.**
and read like this: **den vierzehnten Juni** *or*
den vierzehnten sechsten
The full stop after the figure represents **ten** which is like the English *th* in *4th, 5th, 10th,* etc, or *rd* in *23rd.*

Now read these dates aloud remembering to add the **-ten** (or **-sten** if the number is more than 20) wherever there is a full stop.

(*a*) 5. März	(*d*) 10. Feb	(*g*) 13. 5.	(*j*) 27. 4.
(*b*) 19. Nov	(*e*) 8. Okt	(*h*) 7. 9.	(*k*) 1. 8
(*c*) 21. Jul	(*f*) 30. Jan	(*i*) 12. 5.	(*l*) 28. 10

Wann haben Sie Geburtstag? *When is your birthday?*
Mein Geburtstag ist am ... or **Ich habe am ... Geburtstag.**
And can you say when the birthdays ringed below are?

JAN					
Mo		7	14	21	28
Di	1	8	15	22	29
Mi	2	9	16	23	30
Do	3	10	17	24	31
Fr	4	11	18	25	
Sa	5	12	19	26	
So	6	13	20	27	

FEB					
Mo		4	11	18	25
Di		5	12	19	26
Mi		6	13	20	27
Do		7	14	21	28
Fr	1	8	15	22	
Sa	2	9	16	23	
So	3	10	17	24	

MÄR					
Mo		4	11	18	25
Di		5	12	19	26
Mi		6	13	20	27
Do		7	14	21	28
Fr	1	8	15	22	29
Sa	2	9	16	23	30
So	3	10	17	24	31

APR					
Mo	1	8	15	22	29
Di	2	9	16	23	30
Mi	3	10	17	24	
Do	4	11	18	25	
Fr	5	12	19	26	
Sa	6	13	20	27	
So	7	14	21	28	

MAI					
Mo		6	13	20	27
Di		7	14	21	28
Mi	1	8	15	22	29
Do	2	9	16	23	30
Fr	3	10	17	24	31
Sa	4	11	18	25	
So	5	12	19	26	

JUN					
Mo		3	10	17	24
Di		4	11	18	25
Mi		5	12	19	26
Do		6	13	20	27
Fr		7	14	21	28
Sa	1	8	15	22	29
So	2	9	16	23	30

JUL					
Mo	1	8	15	22	29
Di	2	9	16	23	30
Mi	3	10	17	24	31
Do	4	11	18	25	
Fr	5	12	19	26	
Sa	6	13	20	27	
So	7	14	21	28	

AUG					
Mo		5	12	19	26
Di		6	13	20	27
Mi		7	14	21	28
Do	1	8	15	22	29
Fr	2	9	16	23	30
Sa	3	10	17	24	31
So	4	11	18	25	

SEPT						
Mo		2	9	16	23	30
Di		3	10	17	24	
Mi		4	11	18	25	
Do		5	12	19	26	
Fr		6	13	20	27	
Sa		7	14	21	28	
So	1	8	15	22	29	

OKT					
Mo		7	14	21	28
Di	1	8	15	22	29
Mi	2	9	16	23	30
Do	3	10	17	24	31
Fr	4	11	18	25	
Sa	5	12	19	26	
So	6	13	20	27	

NOV					
Mo		4	11	18	25
Di		5	12	19	26
Mi		6	13	20	27
Do		7	14	21	28
Fr	1	8	15	22	29
Sa	2	9	16	23	30
So	3	10	17	24	

DEZ						
Mo		2	9	16	23	30
Di		3	10	17	24	31
Mi		4	11	18	25	
Do		5	12	19	26	
Fr		6	13	20	27	
Sa		7	14	21	28	
So	1	8	15	22	29	

What date are you arriving and leaving?
Ich komme ... *I'm arriving ...*
Ich fahre ...: *I'm going/leaving ...*

eg. 20. 7-1. 8: **Ich komme am zwanzigsten siebten.**
Ich fahre am ersten achten.

(*a*) 13.07 – 25.07 (*c*) 21.12 – 27.12
(*b*) 16.08 – 3.09 (*d*) 4.03 – 18.03

Dialoge

Sie	Herr Braun
	Gehen wir ins Kino?
Ja, gerne. Wann?	
	Nächste Woche, am Montag? Geht das?
Ja. Um wieviel Uhr?	
	Um sieben Uhr abends.
Gehen wir in die Pizzeria?	
	Ja, gerne. Wann?
Morgen abend?	
	Nein. Das geht leider nicht. Wie wäre es mit Mittwoch abend?
Ja, prima. Um wieviel Uhr?	
	Um halb sieben?
Ja, bis dann. Tschüß.	
Spielen wir heute nachmittag Tennis?	
	Heute habe ich keine Zeit. Wie wäre es mit Samstag?
Ja, gut. Um wieviel Uhr?	
	Um zwei Uhr nachmittags.

Lerntips

- Read both parts of the dialogues.

Übung 2

How would you invite someone to do the following? Note that the day of the week and/or times come earlier in the German sentence:

Example: Go to the theatre with you on Friday evening?
Answer: Gehen wir Freitag abend ins Theater?

(*a*) Play tennis with you on Monday evening.
(*b*) Go to the cinema with you tomorrow evening.
(*c*) Go to the pizzeria with you today at 8 pm.

Now use what you have learned to invite someone to:

(*d*) go swimming (**schwimmen**) Wednesday afternoon.
(*e*) play squash Saturday at 11.00.
(*f*) go to a restaurant (**das Restaurant**) Friday evening.

Übung 3

Frau Fischer invites you to their house that evening. Complete this short conversation.

Fr. Fischer **Kommen Sie heute abend zu uns?**
You *Say you can't make it tonight.*
Fr. Fischer **Oh, das tut mir leid.**
Wann können Sie kommen?
You *Ask if Thursday evening would be all right.*

Übung 4

Rollenspiel: *Role play*
Am Telefon *On the phone*: You are going to visit Herr Braun in Köln. Say your part of the dialogue.

Herr Braun **Hallo. ...... Wie geht's?**
(*a*) *You* *Well, thank you and you?*
Herr Braun **Gut, danke. Wann kommen Sie?**
(*b*) *You* *On Monday, 15th July.*
Herr Braun **Wann kommen Sie in Köln an?**
(When do you get in to Cologne?)
(*c*) *You* *at 18.35.*
Herr Braun **Wann fahren Sie von London ab?**
(When do you leave London?)
(*d*) *You* *At 9.30 am.*
Herr Braun **Wie lange bleiben Sie?**
(How long are you staying?)

(*e*) *You* *Until Friday evening.*
Herr Braun **Um wieviel Uhr fahren Sie ab?**
(*f*) *You* *At 19.30.*
Herr Braun **Wann kommen Sie in London an?**
(*g*) *You* *At 7.30 am.*
Herr Braun **Gut. Ich freue mich schon darauf.**
(*h*) *You* *Goodbye.*
Herr Braun **Auf Wiederhören.**

Kulturtips

Germans like to celebrate their birthdays and often take cakes or buns to work to share with their colleagues on their birthday.

If you are giving flowers as a present you should always buy an odd number and unwrap them as you hand them over.

eine Geburtstagskarte

eine Weihnachtskarte

Wiederholung

1 Making arrangements. **Wann treffen wir uns?** *When shall we meet?* Tell your friend you will see her on:
(*a*) Monday 2nd May at 12.30
(*b*) Friday 24th December at 14.30
(*c*) next Sunday at 11.15
(*d*) next week, on Thursday at 16.30
(*e*) Wednesday 16th April 9.15
(*f*) Saturday 1st September at 17.00
(*g*) next Tuesday at 13.30
(*h*) Friday at 8 p.m.

Höraufgabe 14: Wann treffen wir uns? *When are we meeting?* Note down the times and dates of these eight meetings.

9

DAS ALPHABET

The alphabet

In this unit you will learn how to:

- say the alphabet
- ask someone to spell their name or where they come from
- spell your own name and address
- spell difficult words
- use the correct form of the word 'you'

Wie schreibt man das?
How do you spell it?

Das Alphabet

a – *ah*	b – *bay*	c – *tsay*	d – *day*	e – *ay*	f – *eff*	g – *gay*
h – *hah*	i – *ee*	j – *yot*	k – *kah*	l – *ell*	m – *emm*	n – *enn*
o – *oh*	p – *pay*	q – *koo*	r – *air*	s – *es*	t – *tay*	u – *ooh*
v – *fow*	w – *vay*	x – *icks*	y – *ipsilon*	z – *tset*		

ä – *eh* äu – *oy* ö – *er* ü – *euh* ß – *ess*

*nn = doppel n
ß = s *tset or* scharfes *s*

Aussprachetips

Letters to watch:

a – *ah*
e – *ay*
i – *ee*

v – *fow*
w – *vay*

Lerntips

- Practise saying the alphabet (after the tape if possible) and check your pronunciation.
- Write down the sound of the letters you need to spell your own name and learn them off by heart.
- **Wie schreibt man das?** *How do you spell it?* (*lit: how does one write it?*).
  Practise spelling these names aloud:
  Peter   Martin   Susanne   Ulrike   Florian

Dialog

Sie	Herr Meyer
Wie heißen Sie?	
	Meyer
Wie schreibt man das?	
	M E Y E R
Und wo wohnen Sie Herr Meyer?	
	In Mannheim.
Mit doppel 'n'?	
	Ja.
Wo sind Sie geboren?	
	In Würzburg.
Wie schreibt man das?	
	W Ü R Z B U R G.
Vielen Dank.	
	Nichts zu danken.

Lerntips

- Practise saying both sides of the dialogue.
- Answer these questions yourself:
  Wie heißen Sie? ....
  Wie schreibt man das? ....
  Und wo wohnen Sie? ....
  Wie schreibt man das? ....
- How would you spell these places in German?
  Chipping Norton   Edinburgh   Conwy   Norfolk
  Stratford   York   Waverley   Oxford

Wie heißen Sie? *or* Wie heißt du?

Sprachtips: Sie or Du?

Sie – *you*
There are three words for *you* in German. The most important one to learn is the 'polite' form which you use when addressing people older than yourself and people you don't know very well.
This is the form you have been using so far:
Wie heißen Sie? *What is your name?* (lit: How are you called?)
Wo wohnen Sie? *Where do you live?*
Haben Sie einen Stadtplan? *Have you got a town plan?*
Wie geht es Ihnen? *How do you do?* (lit: How goes it to you?)

Du – *you*
This form is used when talking to a child or someone you know well. You would not normally use it to an adult until they invite you to. If you know someone well they may say:
Duzen wir uns.
This means you should use **du** instead of **Sie**.
Wie heißt du? **Wo wohnst du?** **Hast du einen Stadtplan?**
Wie geht es dir? *How are you?* (lit: How goes it to you?)
If you call each other by your first names you can usually start to use the **du** form.

Ihr – *you*
The third form is the plural of **du**. You use it with a group of children or people that you know well.
(Concentrate on learning the other two forms first and come back to this later when you are more confident with the other two forms.)

Word patterns

When using the **Sie**-form the verb ends with **-en.**
When using **Du**-form the verb ends with **-st.**

Kommen Sie mit dem Auto?	**Spielen Sie Tennis?**
Kommst du mit dem Auto?	**Spielst du Tennis?**
Are you coming by car?	*Do you play tennis?*

Übung 1

Sie form or **Du** form? Find the right form:
You are talking to Frau Schneider. How would you ask her:
(*a*) *How are you?*
(*b*) *When are you coming to London?*
(*c*) *What are you doing tomorrow?*
(*d*) *Do you like playing tennis?*
(*e*) *Do you like swimming?*
(*f*) *Would you like a cup of coffee?*

Übung 2

Now you are talking to Frau Schneider's 13-year-old daughter Melanie. Ask her the same questions, choosing the right ones from those listed below:
(*a*) Wie geht es dir?
(*b*) Was machst du morgen?
(*c*) Wann kommen Sie nach London?
(*d*) Schwimmen Sie gern?
(*e*) Spielst du gern Tennis?
(*f*) Wie geht es dir?
(*g*) Was machst du morgen?
(*h*) Trinkst du gern eine Tasse Kaffee?
(*i*) Trinken Sie gern eine Tasse Kaffee?
(*j*) Wie geht es Ihnen?
(*k*) Was machen Sie morgen?
(*l*) Wann kommst du nach London?
(*m*) Schwimmst du gern?
(*n*) Spielen Sie gern Tennis?
(*o*) Was machen Sie morgen?

Übung 3

Here is Herr Meyer's 12-year-old daughter.
(*a*) You are going to ask her her name.
Which form are you going to use?
(*b*) Ask her how she is.
(*c*) Now ask her if she would like a cup of coffee or a glass of orange juice.

Höraufgabe 15: Which form is being used in each of the sentences you hear?

— An der Rezeption *At reception* —

Schlüsselwörter

Wie schreibt man das?	How do you write it?
Wie buchstabiert man das?	How do you spell it?
Langsamer, bitte.	Slower, please.
der Vorname	first name
der Familienname/Nachname	surname
der Bindestrich	hyphen
der Buchstabe	letter (character)

Listen to (or read) these short conversations:

Wie heißen Sie?

König

Wie schreibt man das?

K Ö N I G

Und mit Vornamen?

Elke

Wie buchstabiert man das?

E L K E

Wie heißt du?

Susanne

Wie schreibt man das?

S U S A N N E

Und wie lautet dein Nachname?

Hoffmann

Mit doppel f?

Ja, und doppel n.

Wie heißen Sie?

Fischer

Wie schreibt man das?

F I S C H E R

Und mit Vornamen?

Hans-Peter

Mit Bindestrich?

Wie heißen Sie?	
	Mein Name ist Kistenmacher.
Wie schreibt man das?	
	K I S T E N M A C H E R
Langsamer bitte!	
	K I S T E N M A C H E R

Lerntips

- Practise reading both parts of the dialogues.

Höraufgabe 16: Wie heißen sie? Write the names of the six people.

Dialog

Empfangsdame	Herr Nabockwicz
Wie heißen Sie?	
	Jürgen Nabockwicz
Wie schreibt man das?	
	NABOCKWICZ
Wie bitte?	
	N A B O C K W I C Z
Woher kommen Sie?	
	Aus Lodz
Wie schreibt man das?	
	LODZ
Langsamer, bitte!	
	L O D Z
Staatsangehörigkeit?	
	Polnisch
Wie ist Ihre Adresse hier in Deutschland?	
	Eichhornweg 63 Dortmund-Applerbeck
Schreibt man das mit Bindestrich?	
	Ja.
Und doppel p?	

	Ja.
Wie ist die Postleitzahl?	
	4600
Und die Telefonnummer?	
	01 23 45
Und die Vorwahl für Dortmund?	
	0230
Unterschreiben Sie hier. Vielen Dank. Auf Wiedersehen.	

Lerntips

- Practise both sides of the conversation.
- Now give your own answers to the receptionist's questions.

Höraufgabe 17: Where do these twelve people live? Write down the details they give.

Wiederholung

1 Welcher Buchstabe fehlt? *Which letter is missing?*

(*a*) Toi.ette
(*b*) Ca.é
(*c*) B.r
(*d*) Restau.ant
(*e*) Ho.el
(*f*) Ba.nhof
(*g*) Stadtzentru.
(*h*) Flu.hafen

2 This little boy is playing with John at the campsite.

(*a*) Ask him his name.
(*b*) Ask where he is from.
(*c*) Would he like a drink of lemonade?

John would like you to ask the little boy to play tennis with him.

(*d*) What are you going to ask?
(*e*) Say at four o'clock.

3 Sie or **Du**? Add the correct ending

(*a*) Was mach.. du morgen?
(*b*) Was mach.. Sie morgen?
(*c*) Wann komm.. Sie nach London?
(*d*) Wann komm.. du nach London?

(*e*) Schwimm.. Sie gern?
(*f*) Schwimm.. du gern?
(*g*) Spiel.. du gern Tennis?
(*h*) Spiel.. Sie gern Tennis?
(*i*) Was mach.. du morgen?
(*j*) Was mach.. Sie morgen?
(*k*) Trink.. du gern eine Tasse Kaffee?
(*l*) Trink.. Sie gern eine Tasse Kaffee?

Schildersprache

Read the letters on these signs (look back at the alphabet on p.86 to check the pronunciation of the letters).

VW BMW

Now see if you can match them up with their meanings!
Volkswagen German car manufacturer
Deutsche Bundesbahn German railways
Bayerische Motorenwerke German car manufacturer
Deutsche Mark German currency
Westdeutscher Rundfunk German radio and TV company
Europäische Gemeinschaft European community
Bundesrepublik Deutschland Federal State of Germany
Gesellschaft mit beschränkter Haftung Limited company (Plc)
Personenkraftwagen car!
die Vereinigten Staaten the United States
Aktiengesellschaft public limited company Plc

ADAC Allgemeiner Deutscher Automobil-Club (AA/RAC equivalent) is pronounced by saying each individual letter: ah-day-ah-say.

Quiz

1 What would you do with a Wiener Schnitzel?
(*a*) wear it (*b*) dance it (*c*) eat it?

2 Who is your Oma?
(*a*) your mother (*b*) your grandmother (*c*) your washing powder?

3 Where would you find the Kölner Dom?
(*a*) in Munich (*b*) in Koblenz (*c*) in Cologne?

4 What would you do with a Schwarzwälder Kirschtorte?
(*a*) not know how to spell it (*b*) not know how to say it (*c*) eat it?

5 Your friend invites you to go to a Kneipe.
(*a*) you say yes (*b*) you ask what time the show begins (*c*) you ask if you should take your swimming costume?

6 Lufthansa is: (*a*) the German national anthem (*b*) the German national airline (*c*) the highest mountain in Germany?

7 You are going to a party and are asked to bring a Lederhose. You would: (*a*) wear it (*b*) eat it (*c*) drink it?

8 What is the English for these towns:
(*a*) München (*b*) Köln (*c*) Stuttgart (*d*) Wien?

9 Which of these are rivers and what are they called in English?
(*a*) der Rhein (*b*) die Mosel (*c*) die Donau (*d*) die Zugspitze?

10 At a party you are offered Glühwein. What should you do with it? (*a*) drink it (*b*) smoke it (*c*) pour it into the nearest plant pot?

11 Tie breaker for the real expert!
There are 16 Länder in the new Germany.
Can you pair the Länder up with their capitals?
(*The new Länder and their capitals have been done already!)

Baden-Württemberg	Saarbrücken
Bayern	Hannover
Berlin	München
*Brandenburg	Potsdam
Bremen	Mainz
Hamburg	Wiesbaden
Hessen	Bremen
*Mecklenburg-Vorpommern	Schwerin
Niedersachsen	Stuttgart
Nordrhein-Westfalen	Hamburg
Rheinland-Pfalz	Berlin
Saarland	Düsseldorf
*Sachsen	Dresden
*Sachsen-Anhalt	Magdeburg
Schleswig-Holstein	Kiel
*Thüringen	Erfurt

10

REFERENCE UNIT:
German Verbs

In this unit you will learn:

- how to identify a verb
- how to know which form of the verb to use
- how to make the correct form of the verb
- how to talk about what is happening (Present tense) and what has happened (Past tense)
- how to look verbs up in the dictionary

This unit does not work in the same way as the preceding and following ones. Do not try to learn everything in it at once. Use it for reference and come back to it as and when you need it.

Verbs are 'doing words': go, sleep, run, eat, talk, think, understand, speak – all things which one can 'do'.
To check if a word is a verb try saying it after:
I ... *or* I can ...
You can learn to speak a language at a simple and effective level by using phrases which you have learned which already include the verb in its correct form eg.
Wie **heißen** Sie? Ich **wohne** in ... Wann **treffen** wir uns?
but there will come a time when you want to say something which you haven't learned and you will want to make up a phrase of your own. To do this you need to learn something more about the patterns of the language.

Look at the pattern of a verb in English:

to make (infinitive)			
(singular)		(plural)	
I	make	we	make
you	make	you	make
he/she/it	make**s**	they	make

Now look at the same verb in German:

machen *to do/to make*			
(singular)		(plural)	
ich	mach**e**	wir	mach**en**
du	mach**st**	ihr	mach**t**
er/sie/es	mach**t**	sie	mach**en**
		Sie	mach**en**
		(you – polite form)	

It is obviously easier to learn an English verb than a German one, because it is the same as the infinitive except that you add an **s** in the *he/she/it* form. (The infinitive is the form of the verb that you will find if you look it up in a dictionary.)

The German verb has seven forms (or persons): (The English verb has six).

The **ich** form, **du** form, **er** form, **wir** form, **ihr** form, **sie** form and **Sie** form.
You already know some of them:

ich	form	– Ich wohn**e**, ich heiß**e**
du	form	– Wann komm**st** du?
wir	form	– Wann treff**en** wir uns?
Sie	form	– Wie heiß**en** Sie?

We are leaving the **ihr**-form out for now. So that leaves us with:

er	form	(he/she it)
sie	form	(they)

Now look at the German verb again and you will find that these two forms are: er/sie/es mach**t** and sie mach**en**.

You make the correct form by taking the **-en** off the infinitive – this gives you the 'stem' of the verb – you then add the ending that you need: -**e**, -**st**, -**t** or -**en**. Here is a short table summarising all the endings:

The **ich** form ends in **e**

The **wir** form ends in **en**
[The **ihr** form ends in **t**]

The **du** form ends in **st**
The **er** form ends in **t**
The **sie** form ends in **en**
The **Sie** form ends in **en**

Übung 1

(*a*) I eat (I am eating) … I am called … I live …
You are talking about yourself so what will the verb end with?
(*b*) What is your name? Where do you live (*you* – polite form)?
You are talking to a stranger so what will the verb end with?
(*c*) What is your name? Would you like a cup of coffee?
You are talking to a younger person so what will the verb end with?
(*d*) You are talking about yourself and someone else (John and I…). Which form will you use? What will the verb end with?

Word patterns

When you are talking about yourself in German the verb almost always ends with an **-e** although it is not always pronounced clearly in spoken German. Remember: **ich** form: **ich …e**

What is the **ich** form of these verbs?

infinitive		**ich** form	
haben	*to have*	**ich ….**	I have
spielen	*to play*	**ich ……**	I play
machen	*to make*	**ich …..**	I make
gehen	*to go*	**ich ….**	I go
schwimmen	*to swim*	**ich ……..**	I swim
essen	*to eat*	**ich ….**	I eat
trinken	*to drink*	**ich …….**	I drink
fahren	*to drive*	**ich …..**	I drive
sehen	*to see*	**ich ….**	I see
kommen	*to come*	**ich …..**	I come

If you know the infinitive it is easy, but what happens when you don't know the word you need? You look it up in the dictionary.

You want to say you will *fetch* the book, so you look up the word *fetch* in the dictionary and this is what it says:

fetch [fetʃ] vt **holen**; (in sale) **einbringen**, **erzielen.**

The word in the brackets [fetʃ] is the phonetic pronunciation of the

English word *fetch*. You know how to pronounce it already so you can ignore this.

You don't want to say how much something fetches in a sale so you can ignore all the second part; the word you want is **holen**. **holen** is the infinitive, so what is the **ich** form going to be?

holen *to fetch* **ich hole** *I fetch*

Try it again. You want to say I'll *bring* the book.
Look up *to bring*:

bring [brɪŋ] vt. irreg. **bringen**; -about **zustande bringen** ...

From 'vt.' you know that it is a verb; irreg. tells you that it is an irregular verb; **bringen** tells you the infinitive of the verb that you want, so you can ignore the rest of the text.
bringen is the infinitive, so the **ich** form will be **ich bringe**.

The Present tense

You use the Present tense to say what you are doing now (or do regularly).

Talking about yourself (I)

Use the **ich**-form, ending in **-e**.

I go	*or*	I am going	**ich gehe**
I eat	*or*	I am eating	**ich esse**
I drink	*or*	I am drinking	**ich trinke**
I go/drive	*or*	I am going/driving	**ich fahre**

gehen means to go when you go on foot;
fahren is used if you go by transport.

Talking about yourself and someone else (we)

Use the **Wir**-form, ending in **-en**.

we go	*or*	we are going	**wir gehen**
we eat	*or*	we are eating	**wir essen**
we drink	*or*	we are drinking	**wir trinken**
we/go drive	*or*	we are going/driving	**wir fahren**

Talking about one other person (he or she)

Use the **Er/sie** -form, ending it **t**.

he/she/it goes	*or*	he/she/it is going	**er/sie geht**
he/she/it eats	*or*	he/she/it is eating	**er/sie ißt**
he/she/it drinks	*or*	he/she/it is drinking	**er/sie trinkt**
he/she/it goes/drives	*or*	he/she/it is going	**er/sie fährt**

essen and **fahren** are irregular verbs which don't always follow the normal pattern.

Talking about more than one other person (they)

Use the **sie**-form, ending in **-en**.

they go	*or*	they are going	**sie gehen**
they eat	*or*	they are eating	**sie essen**
they drink	*or*	they are drinking	**sie trinken**
they go/drive	*or*	they are going/driving	**sie fahren**

Using the du- and Sie-forms

Remember the normal form is the **Sie**-form.
You use the **du**-form only with people you know well and younger people.

Übung 2

Which forms are you going to use?
(*a*) You are talking about your friend Harry.
(*b*) You are talking about yourself and Monika.
(*c*) You are talking about your friends Herr and Frau Schulz.
(*d*) You are asking Herr Braun a question.
(*e*) You are asking his young son a question.
(*f*) You are talking about yourself.

Sprachtips

There are some special verbs which don't end in '**e**' in the **ich**-form. They are:

ich **weiß**	*I know*	ich **will**	*I want to*
ich **bin**	*I am*	ich **darf**	*I may*
ich **kann**	*I can*	ich **soll**	*I should*
ich **mag**	*I like*		

Word patterns: regular verbs and irregular verbs

Regular verbs are ones which follow a special pattern. Unfortunately there are also some irregular verbs which don't always follow the pattern.

Present tense

(What you are doing now or usually do)
English has two forms of the present tense, for example:
I play/I am playing I go/I am going
German only has one, so

Ich spiele means	*I play* as well as	*I am playing.*
Ich gehe means	*I go* as well as	*I am going.*

Past tense

(What you have done or did)
There are two ways of saying, in English, what you did in the past:

Past:	I played	I went
Perfect:	I have played	I have gone

If you were learning English verbs you would have to learn, for example:

Regular verbs:			Irregular verbs:		
Infinitive	*Past*	*Past Participle*	*Infinitive*	*Past*	*Past Participle*
play	played	played	go	went	gone
dance	danced	danced	bring	brought	brought
clean	cleaned	cleaned	drink	drank	drunk
wash	washed	washed	eat	ate	eaten
			swim	swam	swum
			come	came	came

The first column is the infinitive, the second is the past tense and the third is the past participle (the part used after *have* in forming the perfect tense: *I have played*). Another way of talking about what you did in the past in English is to say, *I was playing, I was going*; this is known as the imperfect tense. In German, one form is the equivalent of English past *and* imperfect.

Here are the same verbs in German. Can you work out which is which?

Infinitive	*Past (Imperfect)*	*Past Participle*
trinken	trank	getrunken
waschen	wusch	gewaschen
schwimmen	schwamm	geschwommen
kommen	kam	gekommen
*tanzen	tanzte	getanzt
essen	aß	gegessen
gehen	ging	gegangen
bringen	brachte	gebracht
*spielen	spielte	gespielt
*putzen	putzte	geputzt

*These verbs are regular.

Now what do you think these verbs might mean?
singen sang gesungen
halten hielt gehalten
fallen fiel gefallen
finden fand gefunden

Forming the past tense in German

This is the pattern of a regular verb in German

1 *Infinitive*	**2** *Present* **er**-*form*	**3** *Imperfect* **ich/er**-*form*	**4** *Past Participle*
mach**en**	mach**t**	mach**te**	**ge**mach**t**

How to use this table

1 The first column tells you the infinitive of the verb.

2 The second column tells you the **er**-form in the present tense because the **du** and **er**-forms are sometimes irregular. In the case of this verb it is what you would expect: -**t**

3 The third column tells you how to form the imperfect tense – how to say: I was doing/I was making. Ich machte. (The imperfect tense is usually used to say what was happening when something else happened e.g. I was doing it when I cut myself/I was driving when I hit the wall. It is an 'imperfect' or 'interrupted' action.)

4 The fourth column tells you the past participle of the verb. You need the past participle to make the perfect tense. You add the past participle to *I have* ... **Ich habe gemacht**.

I did it/have done it.	**Ich habe es gemacht.**
I played/have played tennis.	**Ich habe Tennis gespielt.**

Notice how the past participle goes to the end of the phrase.

The **perfect tense** is the one that you use most when talking about what you have done. This is the past tense that you should try to learn first. For this:

Word patterns for past participles

The past participle of a regular verb is made by adding **ge** to the front of the word and using the -**t** ending

machen	**ge** + mach +**t**	**gemacht** *made/did*
kaufen	**ge** + kauf +**t**	**gekauft** *bought*

If you are looking up a word which begins with **ge-** in the dictionary and can't find it, it is probably a past participle. Try taking off the ge- and looking for the rest of the word.

Übung 3

What are the infinitives of these verbs? ie. what should you look up?

(*a*) geholt	(*c*) gearbeitet	(*e*) gesagt
(*b*) gelernt	(*d*) gefragt	(*f*) getanzt

Übung 4

How would you make the past participle of these verbs?

(*a*) hören	(*c*) führen	(*e*) haben
(*b*) brauchen	(*d*) spielen	(*f*) kochen

Irregular verbs

Since most of the verbs in common use are irregular ones (just as in English – and they are usually the same ones as in English as our languages have some of the same origins) there is a list of them in most dictionaries and text books.

There is a list of the most useful ones on page 215 of this book.

This is how irregular verbs are shown in most dictionaries:

1	2	3	4
beginnen	beginnst/beginnt	begann	begonnen – to begin
*bleiben	bleibst/bleibt	blieb	geblieben – to stay
denken	denkst/denkt	dachte	gedacht – to think
essen	ißt/ißt	aß	gegessen – to eat
fahren	fährst/fährt	fuhr	gefahren – to go/drive

[In this case column 2 includes the du- and the er- forms]

How to use the table

1 The infinitive: **beginnen** *to begin.*

2 The present tense: **beginnst/beginnt**. This is what you would expect for the **du** and **er** forms so you know that **beginnen** is regular in the present tense.

3 The imperfect tense: **ich begann** *I was beginning*

4 The past participle (use with ich habe. **ich habe begonnen** *I began/I have begun*

bleiben

1 The infinitive: **bleiben** *to stay, to remain*

2 The present tense: (regular) **du bleibst, er bleibt**

3 The imperfect: **ich blieb** *I was staying* The vowels have changed round: **ei** to **ie**.

4 The past participle **ich bin geblieben** *I stayed/I have stayed*

*The asterisk tells you to use **ich bin** instead of **ich habe**:

I have stayed **ich bin** geblieben.

Übung 5

What is the infinitive of these words? (ie. what would you look up to find out what these words mean?)

(*a*) gelesen (*c*) geschlafen (*e*) gesehen (*g*) gewaschen

(*b*) gegeben (*d*) gerufen (*f*) gefahren

Using sein and haben for the perfect tense

The verbs *to be* and *to have* are called auxiliary verbs as they are used as 'helper' verbs to make other tenses.

The present tense of sein and haben

sein *to be*

ich bin	*I am*	**wir sind**	*we are*
du bist	*you are*	**ihr seid**	*you are*
er/sie/es ist	*he/she/it is*	**sie sind**	*they are*
		Sie sind	*you are (polite form)*

haben *to have*

ich habe	**wir haben**
du hast	**ihr habt**
er/sie/es hat	**sie haben**
	Sie haben

Sein and **haben** are both used to make the perfect tense:

Ich **habe** Squash **gespielt.**
Ich **habe** den Film **gesehen**
Er **hat** Tennis **gespielt.**
Wir **haben** 007 **gesehen.**

Ich **bin** in Hamburg **geblieben.**
Ich **bin** nach Köln **gefahren.**
Sie **ist** in München **geblieben.**
Wir **sind** nach Italien **gefahren.**

✻ **Remember:** you are not supposed to learn everything in this unit at once. Only refer to it as and when you need it.

The main points to remember:

If you are talking about yourself use the **ich**-form: after **ich** the verb ends in **e;**

eg. **Ich** trink**e** ein Glas Bier. *I'm drinking a glass of beer.*

If you are saying what you have done use: **Ich habe/ich bin** + the past participle

Learn this sentence as a model:

Ich bin in die Stadt gefahren und ich habe einen Pullover gekauft.

I went to town and bought a pullover.

(lit: I am in to the town gone and I have a pullover bought).

11

IM HOTEL

In the hotel

In this unit you will learn how to:

- book in to an hotel
- ask where things are
- ask when things are
- ask to pay the bill
- say if anything is wrong
- understand how to use the phone

— An der Rezeption: *at reception* —

Schlüsselwörter

Haben Sie ...?	Have you ...?
das Zimmer	the room
Einzelzimmer	single room
Doppelzimmer	double room
Wie lange?	How long (for)?
die Nacht (die Nächte)	night (nights)
das Bad	bath
die Dusche	shower
das Telefon	the telephone
Wieviel kostet es?	How much does it cost?
das Frühstück	breakfast
Ist Frühstück inbegriffen?	Is breakfast included?
Um wieviel Uhr ...?	At what time?
ab ... bis	from ... to
im dritten Stock	on the third floor
der Fahrstuhl	the lift
dort drüben	over there
bleiben	to stay or remain
Würden Sie sich bitte eintragen?	Would you sign in please?

Lerntips

- Read the German words aloud. How many can you remember?
- Decide which it would be useful to learn and which you will only need to recognise. Look for ways to remember the useful phrases.
- Cover them up and see how many you can remember.

Übung 1

How are you going to ask … *Have you a…?*

(*a*) single room with shower
(*b*) double room with bath
(*c*) single room with bath
(*d*) double room with shower

Übung 2

Can you remember the word for *where*?
How would you ask:

(*a*) Where is the room?
(*b*) Where is the lift?
(*c*) Where is the telephone?

Dialog

Sie	Empfangsdame
Haben Sie ein Zimmer frei?	
	Einzelzimmer oder Doppelzimmer?
Doppelzimmer.	
	Ja. Wie lange bleiben Sie?
Zwei Nächte.	
	Mit Bad oder mit Dusche?
Mit Bad. Wieviel kostet es?	
	70 DM.
Und was kostet ein Zimmer mit Dusche?	
	62 DM.

Ist das Frühstück inbegriffen?

Ja.

Ich nehme das Zimmer mit Dusche.
Um wieviel Uhr ist das Frühstück?

Ab 6.00 Uhr.

Bis wann?

Bis 9.00 Uhr.
Zimmer 307 im dritten Stock.
Der Fahrstuhl ist dort drüben.
Würden Sie sich bitte eintragen?
Hier ist Ihr Schlüssel.

Lerntips

- Make sure you understand all the dialogue.
- Read both parts of the dialogue aloud.
- Cover up the left-hand part and work out what to say.

Höraufgabe 18: Listen to the six customers making their reservations. What sort of rooms do they want? How long are they staying?

Ich möchte ...: I would like ...

What other things might you want to ask or say?
Here are some suggestions.

Haben sie ...	Have you ...
ein Familienzimmer?	a family room?
ein Zweibettzimmer?	a room with twin beds?
ein Dreibettzimmer?	a room with three beds?
etwas Billigeres?	anything cheaper?
eine Garage?	a garage?
ein Zimmer mit Balkon?	a room with a balcony?
ein Zimmer mit Fernseher?	a room with television?
ein Zimmer mit Telefon?	a room with a phone?

Ich möchte ...	I would like to ...
nach England anrufen	ring England
im Zimmer frühstücken	have breakfast in my room
das Fenster öffnen	open the window
die Heizung ausmachen	turn off the heating
zahlen	pay
ein Quittung	a receipt
Gibt es ...	Is there ...
eine Garage?	a garage?
eine Tiefgarage?	an underground garage?
einen Parkplatz?	a car park?
ein Schwimmbad?	a swimming pool?
einen Fitneßraum?	a fitness room?
eine Bar?	a bar?
ein Restaurant?	a restaurant?
ein Telefon im Zimmer?	a telephone in the room?
Ich habe ein Zimmer reserviert.	I have a room booked.
Würden Sie mich um ... wecken?	Would you wake me at ...?
Nehmen Sie (Kredit) Karten?	Do you take (credit) cards.
Unterschreiben Sie hier.	Sign here.

Note that with **der** words **ein** becomes **einen** after **ich möchte** .., **haben Sie** ...?, **gibt es** ... and many other verbs: eg.

Gibt es ein**en** Fitneßraum im Hotel?

Lerntips

- Practise reading all the phrases aloud.
  If possible find someone to read out phrases to you at random and see if you can recognise the meanings.
- Learn the three key phrases:
  Haben Sie ...?
  Ich möchte ...
  Gibt es ...?
- Cover up the German and see how many of the phrases you can remember.

Übung 3

Now you should be ready to complete your part of these dialogues.

(*a*) *You* — *I have a room booked.*
Empfangsherr — **Ihr Name bitte?**
(*b*) *You* — (*Give your name*)

Empfangsherr **Doppelzimmer mit Bad?**

(*c*) *You* *No. Single with shower.*
Empfangsherr **Ach, ja. Zimmernummer 35**

(*d*) *You* *Pardon?*
Empfangsherr **35. Im dritten Stock.**

(*e*) *You* *Is there a lift?*
Empfangsherr **Ja, dort drüben.**

(*f*) *You* *When is breakfast?*
Empfangsherr **Ab 6.00 Uhr.**

(*g*) *You* *Can I have a call at 6.30?*
Empfangsherr **Ja. Hier ist Ihr Schlüssel.**

(*h*) *You* *Have you got a room free?*
Empfangsherr **Ja. Für wie lange?**

(*i*) *You* *For three nights.*
Empfangsherr **Einzelzimmer oder Doppelzimmer?**

(*j*) *You* *Double.*
Empfangsherr **Mit Bad oder Dusche?**

(*k*) *You* *Bath. Is there a telephone in the room?*
Empfangsherr **Ja. und Fernseher.**

(*l*) *You* *How much does it cost?*
Empfangsherr **146 DM pro Nacht.**

(*m*) *You* *Is breakfast included?*
Empfangsherr **Ja.**

(*n*) *You* *Say you would like your bill.*
Empfangsherr **Zimmernummer?**

(*o*) *You* *811. Do you take credit cards?*
Empfangsherr **Ja. Unterschreiben Sie hier.**

(*p*) *You* *A receipt please.*
Empfangsherr **Bitte schön.**

(*q*) *You* *Ask if you can be woken.*
Empfangsherr **Ja, um wieviel Uhr?**

(*r*) *You* *At 6.30 Uhr.*
Empfangsherr **Welche Zimmernummer haben Sie?**

(*s*) *You* *207.*

— Was ist los? *What's wrong?* —

Schlüsselwörter

... funktioniert nicht	... doesn't work
die Heizung	the heating
das Fenster	the window
der Wasserhahn	the water tap
das Licht	the light
die Dusche	the shower
der Schalter	the switch
Das Zimmer ist ...	The room is ...
zu laut.	too noisy.
zu klein.	too small.
zu kalt.	too cold.
zu heiß.	too hot.
zu teuer.	too expensive.
Es gibt kein/keine/keinen ...	There's no ...
kein Telefon.	telephone.
kein Bad.	bath.
keine Bar.	bar.
keinen Fernseher.	TV.
Die Heizung funktioniert nicht.	The heating doesn't work.
Das Licht ist kaputt.	The bulb has gone.
Jemand kommt gleich.	Someone is coming straight away.
Welche Zimmernummer haben Sie?	What is your room number?
Wie funktioniert ...?	How does ... work?
Ich nehme es.	I'll take it.
der Zimmerservice	room service
Ich habe meinen Schlüssel verloren.	I have lost my key.

Lerntips

- Learn the four key phrases:
  ... funktioniert nicht
  Das Zimmer ist zu ...
  Es gibt kein ...
  Wie funktioniert ...?

Bitte das
Zimmer aufräumen
*****
Please make up
the room
*****
Priére de faire
la chambre de suite
Bitte nicht stören!
.....
Please don't disturb!
.....
Priére de ne pas
deranger!

Übung 4

Now try these dialogues.

(*a*) *You*	*Excuse me please.*
Empfangsdame	**Bitte?**
(*b*) *You*	*My room is too noisy.*
Empfangsdame	**Das tut mir leid. Zimmer 14 ist frei aber es gibt kein Bad.**
(*c*) *You*	*Is there a shower?*
Empfangsdame	**Ja.**
(*d*) *You*	*I'll take it.*
Empfangsdame	**Hier ist der Schlüssel. Im ersten Stock, links.**
(*e*) *You*	*Excuse me please.*
Empfangsdame	**Bitte?**
(*f*) *You*	*My room is too hot. How does the heating work?*
Empfangsdame:	**Es gibt einen Schalter unter dem Fenster.**

Am Telefon

(*g*) *You*	*Room service?*
Empfangsdame	**Ja.**
(*h*) *You*	*The light bulb has gone.*
Empfangsdame	**Jemand kommt gleich. Welche Zimmernummer haben Sie?**
(*i*) *You*	*48.*
(*j*) *You*	*Room service?*
Empfangsdame	**Ja.**
(*k*) *You*	*Can you wake me at 6.30?*
Empfangsdame	**Welche Zimmernummer haben Sie?**
(*l*) *You*	*63. I would like breakfast in my room.*
Empfangsdame	**Um wieviel Uhr?**
(*m*) *You*	*7 am.*

Practise asking for the items shown.

Ich möchte ... *I would like ...*

Ich brauche ...	*I need ...*
Es gibt kein/e/en ...	*There isn't a ...*
Wo kann ich hier ... kaufen?	*Where can I get a ...?* *(lit: Where can I here ... buy?)*

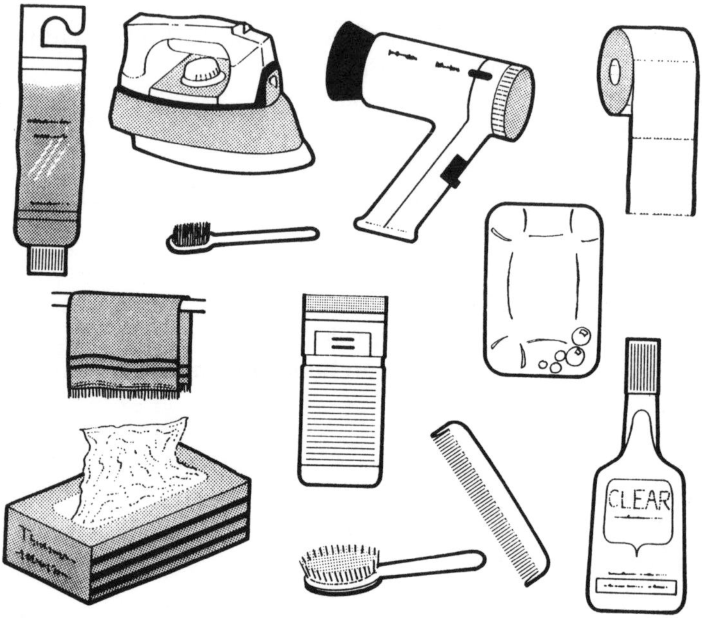

Ich möchte nach England anrufen: *I want to ring England*

Schlüsselwörter

Sie wählen	you dial
zuerst	first
und dann	and then
das Ortsgespräch	local call
das Ferngespräch	long distance call
anrufen	to call
drücken	to press
die schwarze Taste	the black key

Word patterns: word order

When you say *I want to do something* and use **Ich möchte** the other verb goes to the end of the sentence.
Ich möchte nach Amerika **anrufen**
Ich möchte nach Frankreich **fahren.**
Ich möchte Tennis mit Hilda **spielen**

Übung 5

Complete the dialogue below:

(*a*) *Say you want to ring England.*

Sie wählen zuerst 0 und dann die Vorwahl für England; 0044

(*b*) *Now say you want to ring room Number 25.*

Sie wählen die Nummer 25.

(*c*) *Ring reception and ask how to make a local call.*

Sie drücken die schwarze Taste und wählen die Nummer.

Tell your German friend how to ring Germany from your home. (The code for German is 010 49.)

Please inform the reception if you are expecting a call and won't be in your room.

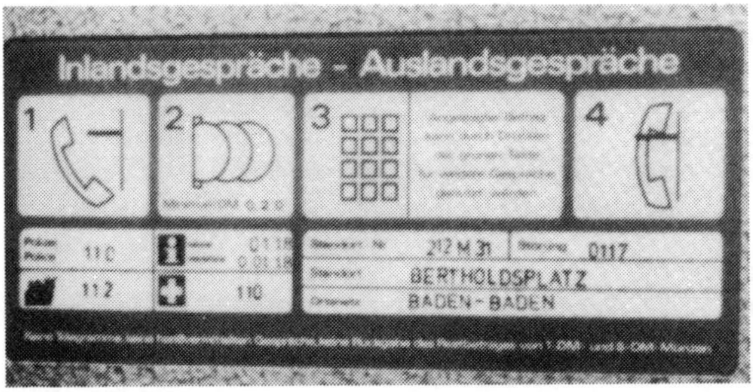

Geld einwerfen – *put in your money (lit: money insert)*

12

MEINE FAMILIE

My family

In this unit you will learn how to:

- talk about your family
- make plural forms
- say what people are like
- say what your job is
- say what jobs other do

Meine Familie: *my family*

Schlüsselwörter

meine Verwandten	my relations
mein ...	my ...
Vater	father
Vati	dad
Stiefvater	stepfather
Schwiegervater	father-in-law
Großvater	grandfather
Opa	grandad
Urgroßvater	great-grandfather
Bruder	brother
Sohn	son
Onkel	uncle
Patenonkel	godfather
Cousin	cousin
Mann	husband
Freund	friend (male)
meine ...	my ...
Mutter	mother
Mutti	mum

Stiefmutter	step-mother
Schwiegermutter	mother-in-law
Großmutter	grandmother
Oma	grandma
Urgroßmutter	great-grandmother
Schwester	sister
Tochter	daughter
Tante	aunt
Patentante	godmother
Cousine	cousin
Frau	wife
Freundin	friend (female)

Aussprachetips

Cousin [cooseng], **Cousine** [cooseenuh],
ie = **ee**, **ei** = **eye**, **ur**- sounds **oor**,
w sounds **v**, **Sohn** sounds **zone**

Word patterns

To say *my father* you use **mein** Vater;
to say *my mother* you use **meine** Mutter;
to say *my parents* you say **meine** Eltern.
Use **mein** with masculine (and neuter) words
meine with feminine words and with plural words.

Lerntip

- Choose the words you will need to talk about your family and try to learn them.

Übung 1

How do you say:

(*a*) my father
(*b*) my sister
(*c*) my grandfather
(*d*) my parents
(*e*) my girl-friend
(*f*) my mother
(*g*) my brother
(*h*) my grandmother
(*i*) my wife
(*j*) my husband
(*k*) my son
(*l*) my daughter
(*m*) my gran
(*n*) my grandad
(*o*) my mother-in-law

Dialoge

Herr Fischer introduces you to his family:

Sie	Herr Fischer
	Darf ich meine Frau vorstellen?
Sehr angenehm.	
	Und das ist meine Tochter Angelika.
Hallo, Angelika.	
	Mein Sohn Peter
Hallo, Peter.	
	Und das ist meine Mutter.
Guten Tag, Frau Fischer.	

and you introduce Herr Fischer to your boss:

Darf ich meinen Chef vorstellen? **Herr Smith – Herr Fischer.**	
	Sehr angenehm.
Haben Sie eine gute Reise gehabt?	
	Ja, danke.

Haben Sie eine gute Reise gehabt?	Did you have a good journey?

Höraufgabe 19: Hannelore, Joachim and Katrin describe their family holiday photos. Which relatives are in the photos? Cross out the ones they mention.

(*a*) Vater Mutter Großmutter Großvater Bruder Schwester Sohn Tochter Hund

(*b*) Vater Mutter Großmutter Großvater Bruder Schwester Sohn Tochter Hund

(*c*) Vater Mutter Großmutter Großvater Bruder Schwester Sohn Tochter Hund

Übung 2

Darf ich meine Familie vorstellen? – May I introduce my family?
Tell your friend Uschi who these people are!
Hier ist …

Word patterns

If you have more than one…

singular	*plural*
mein Bruder	meine Brüder
meine Schwester	meine Schwestern
mein Sohn	meine Söhne
meine Tochter	meine Töchter

The changes needed to make the plural form are usually shown in brackets after the noun in the vocabulary or in a dictionary, for example:

- **der Bruder (¨)** means that you add an Umlaut to the u to form the plural: **zwei Brüder.**

- **die Schwester (n)** means that you add an **'n'** to form the plural: **eine Schwester, zwei Schwestern.**
- **das Fenster (-)** [window] means that the word doesn't change in the plural: **ein Fenster, zwei Fenster.**

In most dictionaries, if you want to find the plural form you will have to look up the word in the singular in the German-English section; it will not be listed in the English-German section.

Übung 3

How do you make the plurals of these words?

(*a*) Tochter (¨) *daughter*
(*b*) der Tisch *table*
(*c*) der Stuhl (¨e) *chair*
(*d*) das Haus (¨er) *house*

Describing people

Schlüsselwörter

ziemlich	rather
ganz	quite
sehr	very
nett	nice
groß/klein	big/small
lang/kurz	long/short
hell/dunkel	light/dark
schlank/dick	thin/fat
schulterlang	shoulder length
lockig	curly
blau	blue
grün	green
grau	grey
weiß	white
rot	red
schwarz	black
braun	brown
Mein Mann ist ziemlich groß.	My husband is rather tall.
Meine Frau ist ganz klein.	My wife is quite small.
45 Jahre alt	45 years old
sehr nett	very nice
Er/sie trägt eine Brille.	He/she wears glasses.
Contaktlinsen.	contact lenses.
Er/sie hat blau/grüne/braune Augen.	He/she has blue/green/brown eyes.

Aussprachetips

ziemlich – [tseemlich] **klein** – [kline]
e at end of a word is always pronounced and sounds -uh

Word patterns

Descriptive words (adjectives) all add an **e** when used in front of a plural word. **Haare** is frequently plural in German (unless you literally mean a single hair), so the adjectives describing someone are plural too, with an **-e**:

Er	hat	lange	blonde	Haare
Sie		kurze	dunkle	
		schulterlange	lockige	

Übung 4

Wie sehen sie aus? Tick the correct statements:

(*a*)

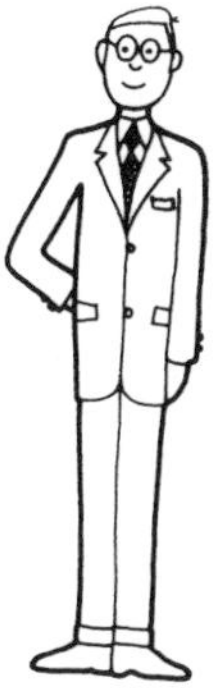

(*b*)

(*a*)

(*i*) Er ist groß.
(*ii*) Er ist klein.
(*iii*) Er hat lange Haare.
(*iv*) Er hat kurze Haare.
(*v*) Er trägt eine Brille.
(*vi*) Er hat dunkle Haare.
(*vii*) Er hat blonde Haare.

(*b*)

(*i*) Sie ist groß.
(*ii*) Sie ist klein.
(*iii*) Sie hat lange Haare.
(*iv*) Sie hat kurze Haare.
(*v*) Sie trägt eine Brille.
(*vi*) Sie hat dunkle Haare.
(*vii*) Sie hat blonde Haare.

Kulturtips

German people usually know exactly how tall they are and will usually tell you they are 1,74m etc rather than say **ganz groß**. Find out how tall you are (in metric measurements!) and learn to say it in German.

Was sind Sie von Beruf?
What job do you do?

Schlüsselwörter

Was sind Sie von Beruf?	What job do you do? (lit: what are you by job?)
der Beruf	job
arbeiten	to work
Ich arbeite (als) ...	I work as ...
Ich bin/er ist/sie ist	I am/he is/she is
Ich bin selbständig.	I am self-employed.
arbeitslos.	unemployed.
der Lehrer	teacher
der Student	student
der Ingenieur	engineer
der Mechaniker	mechanic
der Verkäufer	salesman
der Polizist	policeman
der Zahnarzt	dentist
der Arzt	doctor
der Politiker	politician
der Programmierer	computer programmer
der Schauspieler	actor
der Moderator	radio/TV presenter
der Kellner	waiter
der Vertreter	sales rep

Word patterns

All the above 'job' words make the feminine form by adding -**in**; eg. **Arzt** also adds an Umlaut: der Arzt, die **Ä**rzt**in;** der Sekretär, die Sekretär**in**

Note that some jobs end in -**mann**. These usually change their ending to -**frau** if the person is a woman, and to **Leute** if there is more than one:

der Mann – *man*	die Frau – *woman*	*businessman/woman*
der Geschäftsmann	die Geschäftsfrau	*buyer/salesperson*
der Kaufmann	die Kauffrau	

die Leute – *people*
die Geschäftsleute – *business people*
also:
der Frisör/Friseur die Frisöse/Friseuse *hairdresser*

An **-in** ending usually means that a word is feminine.
Der Freund is a friend (male); **die Freundin** is a (female) friend. **der Journalist** is a male journalist, so a female one is **die Journalistin.**

Lerntips

- Read the words out aloud.
- Select the ones which you think you would find most useful and learn them.

Dialog Ich bin ...: I am ...

Sie	Fräulein Fischer
	Was sind Sie von Beruf?
Ich bin Autoelektriker.	
	Was ist Fräulein Smith von Beruf?
Sie ist Krankenpflegerin.	
	Und was macht Herr Black?
Er ist Tischler.	
	Was machen Herr und Frau Shaw?
Er ist Elektriker und sie hilft ihm im Geschäft.	
	Was macht ihre Tochter?
Sie ist Buchhändlerin. Sie arbeitet bei einer kleinen Firma.	
	Was macht ihr Sohn?
Er ist Graphiker aber er ist im Moment arbeitslos.	

Lerntips

- Read the dialogue aloud.
- There are some new words:

(*a*) Krankenpflegerin (*c*) Elektriker (*e*) Graphiker.
(*b*) Tischler (*d*) Buchhändlerin

Cross out the ones you already know or can guess. See how many of the clues you need to get the other ones!

(*a*) **Kranken** *the sick*, **pflegen** *to look after*, so
Krankenpflegerin *a nurse* (female)

(*b*) **der Tisch** *the table*,
they used to be made out of wood, so
der Tischler, *joiner*

(*c*) **der Elektriker** *electrician*

(*d*) **das Buch** *the book*,
handeln *to trade*, so
der Buchhändler/die Buchhändlerin *bookseller*

(*e*) **der Graphiker** *graphic designer*

- Now re-read the dialogue substituting your family or friends and saying what jobs they do.

Schlüsselwörter

arbeiten	to work
Ich arbeite als ...	I work as a ...
der Arbeiter/-in	the worker
arbeitslos	without work (unemployed)
der Arbeitgeber	employer (work giver)
der Arbeitnehmer	employee (work taker)
das Arbeitsamt	employment exchange
das Amt	office

Word patterns

Talking about yourself – the verb ends with **-e**

I work	ich arbeit**e**

Talking about other people – the verb ends with **-t**

he works	er arbeite**t**
she works	sie arbeite**t**

Talking about yourself and someone else **-en**
we work wir arbeit**en**
Talking about two or more people **-en**
they work sie arbeit**en**

Word building – building up your vocabulary

Arbeit(s-) means *work* and **die Kleidung** means *clothes*
der Platz means *place*.

So, using the word-building principle it's easy to work out how you would say work clothes and workplace: **die Arbeitskleidung, der Arbeitsplatz.**

Remember that the gender of the new noun is the same as that of the last word.

Übung 5

What new words can you make with Arbeits- and these words?

(*a*) der Beginn *beginning*
(*b*) die Pause *break*
(*c*) das Zimmer *room*
(*d*) das Ende *end*
(*e*) der Tisch *table*
(*f*) die Zeit *time*
(*g*) die Woche *week*
(*h*) der Schluß *end*
(*i*) der Vertrag *contract*

Practise saying your new words.

Übung 6

Using the following vocabulary clues, can you make the German equivalents of the English (a) – (d)?

die Post *post*; **das Amt** *office*;
Verkaufs *sales*; **das Büro** *office*;
Reise- *travel*; **Auskunfts-** *information*.

(*a*) sales office
(*b*) information office
(*c*) Post Office
(*d*) travel agency

Übung 7

Here are Herr Braun and Silke Müller. Which questions would be suitable to ask each of them, and which replies belong to which person?

(*a*) Was sind Sie von Beruf?
(*b*) Was machst du?
(*c*) Wo arbeitest du?
(*d*) Wo arbeiten Sie?
(*e*) Was machen Sie?
(*f*) Was bist du ...?
(*g*) Ich bin Studentin.
(*h*) Bei BMW.
(*i*) Ich bin Motormechaniker.
(*j*) Auf einer Hotelfachschule.

Höraufgabe 20: What do these eight people do for a living?

13

EINKAUFEN

Shopping

In this unit you will learn how to:

- find your way around the shops
- ask for things in shops
- buy presents and souvenirs
- buy clothes
- ask about sizes, materials and colours
- ask to try something on

Die Läden: *the shops*

Schlüsselwörter

There are two words (often interchangeable) for shop:
das Geschäft – shop (or business)
der Laden – shop

die Apotheke	(dispensing) chemist
die Bäckerei	bakery
das Blumengeschäft	florist
die Buchhandlung	bookshop
die Drogerie	chemist (not dispensing)
das Elektrogeschäft	electrical goods
das Fotogeschäft	photographer's
der Geschenkladen	gift shop
der Gemüseladen	greengrocer's
das Kaufhaus	department store
die Konditorei	cake shop
die Metzgerei	butcher's
die Reinigung	cleaner's
der Schreibwarenladen	stationer's

das Schuhgeschäft	shoe shop
der Souvenirladen	souvenir shop
der Supermarkt	supermarket
der Tabakhändler	tobacconist
der Tante-Emma-Laden	corner shop (lit: Aunt Emma's shop)
der Zeitungskiosk	newspaper shop
Wo ist hier ein Supermarkt?	Is there a supermarket near here? (lit: Where is here a supermarket?)

Übung 1

Which shop would you go to?

Wo kann ich hier ... kaufen?
Where can I buy?

Schlüsselwörter

Andenken	souvenirs
Blumen	flowers
Briefpapier/Schreibpapier	writing paper
Briefmarken	stamps
Brot	bread
ein Buch	a book
eine CD/Compact Disc	a compact disc
einen Film	a film
ein Geschenk	a present
einen Kuchen	a cake
einen Mantel	a coat
Medikamente	medicine
ein Paar Schuhe	a pair of shoes
eine Zahnbürste	a toothbrush
Zahnpasta	toothpaste
Zigaretten	cigarettes
eine Flasche Parfüm	a bottle of perfume
eine Flasche Wein	a bottle of wine
Weingläser	wine glasses
einen Bierkrug	a beer mug
eine Schale	a scarf
Ohrringe	earrings

Übung 2

What do you think they might be buying? Fill in a suitable word and then practise the dialogues.
(**Passantin** *passer-by*)

Touristin **Wo kann ich hier einen (*a*) ... kaufen?**
Passant **Das Fotogeschäft ist hier gleich um die Ecke.**

Touristin **Ich möchte eine (*b*) ... Gibt es ein Musikgeschäft hier in der Nähe?**

Touristin **Wo kann ich (*c*) ...... kaufen?**
Passantin **Die Post ist in der Hauptstraße neben dem Bahnhof. Aber es gibt einen Zeitungskiosk gleich hier.**

Touristin	**Ich brauche (*d*) ......**
Passant	**Die Drogerie ist neben der Bäckerei.**

Kulturtips

As well as at the Post Office you can usually buy stamps anywhere that sells picture postcards and at most newsagents and tobacconists (who usually sell tickets for local transport).

In an **Apotheke** you can get a prescription made up, but you can also buy medication without a prescription and the **Apotheke** is qualified to suggest remedies for most minor ailments.

Im Geschäft: *In the shop*

Schlüsselwörter

Haben Sie ...?	Have you ...?
Ich möchte ...	I would like ...
Ich nehme ...	I'll take ...
Ich brauche	I need ...
Ich suche ...	I am looking for ...
Wieviel kostet ...?	How much does ... cost?
etwa	about
Haben Sie etwas Billigeres?	Have you anything cheaper?
Kann ich Ihnen helfen?	Can I help you?
Sonst noch etwas?	Anything else?
ein Geschenk für	a present for
meinen Mann	my husband
meine Frau	my wife
meinen Bruder/meine Schwester	my brother/sister
meinen Vater/meine Mutter	my father/mother
meinen Freund/meine Freundin	my friend, boyfriend/girlfriend
meinen Sohn/meine Tochter	my son/daughter
Könnten Sie es/sie als Geschenk einpacken?	Could you pack it/them as a present?

Übung 3

You want to buy presents for your family and friends. How would you say *I am looking for a present for ...*
Ich suche ein Geschenk für ...

(*a*) my girl-friend
(*b*) my brother
(*c*) my grand-mother
(*d*) my wife
(*e*) my husband
(*f*) my mother
(*g*) my boy-friend
(*h*) my son

Übung 4

(*a*) Ask if they have:
 (*i*) a book
 (*ii*) writing paper
 (*iii*) a bottle of perfume
(*b*) Say you're looking for:
 (*i*) a bottle of wine
 (*ii*) wineglasses
 (*iii*) a beer mug
(*c*) Say you'd like:
 (*i*) a scarf
 (*ii*) earrings
 (*iii*) a cake

Kulturtips

A gift-wrapping service is offered free in most German shops. You will usually be asked:

Soll ich das als Geschenk einpacken? — *Shall I gift-wrap it for you?*
Soll ich den Preis abmachen? — *Shall I take the price off?*

Dialog

Sie	Verkäuferin
	Kann ich Ihnen helfen?
Ich möchte ein Geschenk für meine Tochter.	
	Wie alt ist sie?
Zwei Jahre.	
	Wie wäre es mit einem Stofftier?

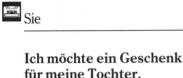

Wieviel kosten sie?

Von etwa 30 DM bis 200 DM.

Wieviel kostet der Teddybär?

Der kleine Bär kostet 24 DM und der große kostet 65 DM. Der Hund kostet 42 DM und die Katze 38 DM.

Ich nehme die Katze. Könnten Sie es als Geschenk einpacken?

Ja, natürlich. Sonst noch etwas?

Haben Sie Computerspiele?

Ja. Skifahrer – das ist neu.

Wieviel kostet es?

46 DM.

Haben Sie etwas Billigeres?

Ja, Autocops. 22 DM.

Ich nehme es.

Sonst noch etwas?

Nein, danke, das ist alles.

Was macht das?

60 DM.

Bitte schön.

Danke. Auf Wiedersehen.

Auf Wiedersehen.

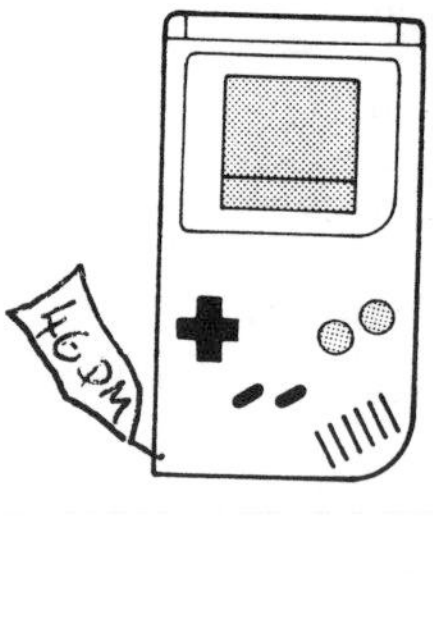

Lerntips

- Read the dialogue and make sure you understand everything.
- Read it aloud. Then cover up the left-hand side and improvise your part of the dialogue to fit.

Höraufgabe 21: What are these six customers buying, and for whom?

Im Kaufhaus: *in the department store*

Schlüsselwörter

einen Pullover	a jumper
eine Hose	trousers (lit: a trouser)
einen Schal	a scarf
ein Paar Handschuhe	a pair of gloves
einen Schlips	a tie
ein Hemd	a shirt
eine Bluse	a blouse
einen Rock	a skirt
einen Anzug	a suit
einen Schlafanzug	pyjamas (lit: a sleeping suit)
ein Kleid	a dress
einen Jogginganzug	a track suit
einen Badeanzug	a swim suit
einen Mantel	a coat
die Farben	colours
rot	red
rosarot	pink
blau	blue
grün	green
grau	grey
schwarz	black
weiß	white
dunkelblau	dark blue
hellblau	light blue
türkis	turquoise
violett	purple
gelb	yellow
braun	brown
bunt	colourful

einfarbig	plain (lit: one-coloured)
gemustert	patterned
kariert	check
aus ...	made of ...
Wolle	wool
Baumwolle	cotton
Leder	leather
Seide	silk
die Größe	size
eine Bluse Größe 36	a blouse size 36
das ist zu teuer	that's too expensive
Ich nehme es/sie	I'll take it/them
Was für ...?	What kind of ...?

Lerntips

- Read all the new words aloud. Select the ones you think would be the most useful to you and learn them.

Übung 5

How would you ask for:

(*a*) a blue jumper size 38?
(*b*) a red blouse size 34?
(*c*) a brown trouser size 36?
(*d*) a green wool scarf?
(*e*) a pair of black gloves?
(*f*) a white cotton shirt?

Women's Coats, Suits, Dresses, and Blouses	**British**	10	12	14	16	18	20		
	American	8	10	12	14	16	18		
	Italian	44	46	48	50	52	54		
	French	40	42	44	46	48	50		
Women's Shoes	**British**	3	4	5	6	7	8	9	
	American	4½	5½	6½	7½	8½	9½	10½	
	Continental	35	36	37	38	39	40	41	
Men's Coats Jackets and Suits	**British**	34	36	38	40	42	44		
	American	34	36	38	40	42	44		
	Continental	44	46	48	50	52	54		
Men's Shoes	**British**	6	7	8	9	10	11		
	American	7	8	9	10	11	12		
	Continental	39½	40½	41½	42½	43½	44½		
Men's Shirts	**British**	14	14½	15	15½	16	16½	17	17½
	American	14	14½	15	15½	16	16½	17	17½
	Continental	36	37	38	39	40	41	42	43

Übung 6

You are buying various items in a branch of the department store Karstadt. Complete your part of the dialogue.

(*a*)	*You*	*You would like to buy a scarf for your mother.*
Verkäuferin		**Welche Farbe?**
(*b*)	*You*	*Blue.*
Verkäuferin		**Dunkelblau oder hellblau?**
(*c*)	*You*	*Dark blue.*
Verkäuferin		**Dieser Schal ist sehr schön.**
(*d*)	*You*	*Is it wool?*
Verkäuferin		**Ja, natürlich. 100 prozentig.**
(*e*)	*You*	*How much does it cost?*
Verkäuferin		**85 DM.**
(*f*)	*You*	*That's a bit expensive.* *Ask if they have anything cheaper.*
Verkäuferin		**Der karierte Schal kostet 46 DM.**
(*g*)	*You*	*You'll take it.*

Now you want a pair of gloves for your friend.

(*h*)	*You*	*Say you'd like a pair of gloves.*
Verkäuferin		**Was für Handschuhe?**
(*i*)	*You*	*Black, leather.*
Verkäuferin		**Welche Größe?**
(*j*)	*You*	*You don't know.*
Verkäuferin		**Groß oder mittelgroß?**
(*k*)	*You*	*Big.*
Verkäuferin		**Die kosten 67 DM.**
(*l*)	*You*	*Say you'll take them. And ask her to gift wrap them.*
Verkäuferin		**Natürlich.**

Now you want a road map (**eine Straßenkarte**)

(*m*)	*You*	*Have you got a road map?*
Verkäuferin		**In der Buchabteilung.**
(*n*)	*You*	*Where is the book section.*
Verkäuferin		**Im vierten Stock.**
(*o*)	*You*	*Ask where the lift is.*
Verkäuferin		**Dort drüben.**
(*p*)	*You*	*Say thank you.*

Höraugabe 22: What are these six customers buying?

Übung 7 Word building

Look at these vocabulary clues and reminders and work out the meaning of the words and signs below.

kaufen	to buy
das Kaufhaus	department store
einkaufen	to shop (lit. to buy in)
verkaufen	to sell
der Verkäufer (die Verkäuferin)	sales assistant
der Kaufmann/die Kauffrau	businessman/woman, trader
der Einzelhandelskaufmann	retailer
der Großhandelskaufmann	wholesaler
der Schluß	end

(*a*) eine Einkaufstasche
(*b*) eine Einkaufsliste
(*c*) Ein Einkaufswagen
(*d*) das Einkaufszentrum

(*e*) Ausverkauf

(*f*) Zu Verkaufen

(*g*) Winterschlußverkauf

(*h*) Sommerschlußverkauf

Sprachtips

Here are some more useful phrases to do with shopping:
Ich kaufe ... *I am buying*
Ich kaufe ein ... *I am shopping*
Ich mache die Einkäufe *I do the shopping*
(lit: I make the purchases)
Ich habe gekauft *I have bought*
Ich habe einen Mantel gekauft *I have bought a coat.*
Notice the word order in the last example. *I have a coat bought.*

Übung 8

Untergeschoß

Autozubehör
Werken und Basteln

Erdgeschoß

Lederwaren
Schreibwaren
Tabakwaren
Bonbons
Kosmetik
Schmuck
Herrenbekleidung

1 Obergeschoß

Kinder – und Damenbekleidung

2 Obergeschoß

Restaurant / Cafe
Reisebüro
WC

3 Obergeschoß

Sportartikel
Sportkleidung
Schwimmsport
Sportschuhe

4 Obergeschoß

Buchhandlung
Musikgeschäft
Elektrogeshaft

Schmuck	jewellery
Autozubehör	car accessories
Werken und Basteln	handicrafts and model building

On which floor would you find...?

(*a*) leather goods
(*b*) books
(*c*) trainers
(*d*) records
(*e*) men's clothing
(*f*) children's clothing
(*g*) car parts
(*h*) tennis rackets
(*i*) model aircraft
(*j*) toilets
(*k*) confectionery
(*l*) ladies' clothing

14

WANN FÄHRT DER ZUG?

When does the train leave?

In this unit you will learn about:

- using public transport in Germany
- asking for travel information
- buying tickets
- reading the signs at the station
- what's in a name?

Am Bahnhof: *at the station*

Schlüsselwörter

der Zug	the train
mit dem Zug	by train
der Bus	the bus
mit dem Bus	by bus
Wann?	When?
das Gleis	platform
fahren	to go
ab/fahren	to depart
kommen	to come
an/kommen	to arrive
um	at
ab von	from
Wann fährt der Zug ab?	When does the train leave?
Um wieviel Uhr fährt der Zug?	At what time does the train leave?
Wann kommt er in München an?	When does it arrive in Munich? (lit: When comes he in Munich in?)
Wo fährt der Zug nach München ab?	Where does the Munich train leave from?
Wann kommt der Bus aus London an?	When does the bus from London arrive?

Word patterns in questions

Look at the word order in the questions:

Wann **fährt** der Zug?	*lit: When **goes** the train?*
Wie **schreibt** man das?	*How **write** you that?*
Wie **geht** es Ihnen?	*How **goes** it to you?*
Wo **wohnen** Sie?	*Where **live** you?*

Sprachtips

Nach usually means *after* as in **Nachmittag** *afternoon*, but it means *to* in expressions like **nach München, nach Italien.**

Übung 1

Put the words in each of these sentences in the right order.

(*a*) der Zug in München wann kommt an?
(*b*) ab der Zug wann fährt?
(*c*) man schreibt wie das?
(*d*) wie es Ihnen geht?
(*e*) Sie wohnen wo?

Übung 2

How would you say ...?

(*a*) to Munich
(*b*) to Italy
(*c*) from England
(*d*) from London

Dialog

Sie	Bahnbeamter
Wann fährt der Zug nach Hamburg?	
	Der nächste Zug nach Hamburg fährt um 11.10.
Wann kommt er in Hamburg an?	
	Um 14.46 Uhr.
Wo fährt er ab?	
	Ab Gleis 7.

Und der nächste Zug nach Köln?

Der fährt um 11.39.

Wann kommt er in Köln an?

Um 16.27.

Wo fährt er ab?

Ab Gleis 14.

Abfahrt

Ankunft

Aussprachetips

ab sounds **ap**
nächste [next-uh]
fährt [fair-t]
Köln [curl-n]

Lerntips

- Read the dialogue and check that you can understand everything
- Practise reading it aloud.
- Cover up the left-hand side. Remember, you want information about the trains to Hamburg and Köln. What questions are you going to ask?
- Now cover up the right-hand side. Here is the information that you need to complete the dialogue. See if you can do it.
  The train to Hamburg leaves at 12.15 from platform 8 and gets in at 15.13. The train to Köln leaves at 14.05 from platform 2 and gets in at 17.44.

Einmal nach Köln, bitte
A ticket to Cologne, please

Schlüsselwörter

die Fahrkarte	the ticket
der Fahrplan	the timetable
die Auskunft	information
die Abfahrt	departure(s)
die Ankunft	arrival(s)
der Bahnsteig	the platform
das Gleis	the track, platform
der Fahrkartenschalter	the ticket office
Schließfächer	(left luggage) lockers
das Gepäck	the luggage
der Koffer	the suitcase
der Kofferkuli	the luggage trolley
der Speisewagen	the dining car
der Schlafwagen	the sleeping car
erste/zweite Klasse	first/second class
Raucher/Nichtraucher	smoker/non-smoker
Ich möchte ...	I would like ...
einen Platz reservieren	to reserve a seat
eine Rückfahrkarte	a return ticket
einmal einfach nach Hamburg	a single to Hamburg
zweimal nach Bonn, hin und zurück	2 returns to Bonn
zweieinhalb	two-and-a-half, i.e. 2 adults, 1 child
anderthalb	one-and-a-half, i.e. 1 adult, 1 child
einsteigen	to get on
umsteigen	to change
aussteigen	to get off
Ich steige in Hamburg ein.	I get on in Hamburg.
Ich steige in Köln um.	I change in Cologne.
Ich steige in Stuttgart aus.	I get off at Stuttgart.
Was kostet es?	how much is it?
Ist dies der Zug nach Trier?	Is this the train for Trier?
Hat der Zug nach Dortmund Verspätung?	Is the Dortmund train late?
Muß ich umsteigen?	Do I have to change?
Wo muß ich umsteigen?	Where do I have to change?

Übung 3

How would you ask for:

(*a*) 1 single to Berlin?
(*b*) 1 return to Salzburg?
(*c*) 3 returns to Mannheim?
(*d*) 2 returns to Koblenz?
(*e*) 2 singles to Osnabrück?
(*f*) 1 return to Innsbruck?

Kulturtips

A **Zuschlag** *supplement* is payable on all IC trains and on D trains for a journey under 50km.
Zuschlagpflichtig means you have to pay a supplement.
You usually have to put your ticket into an **Entwerter** to get the date stamped on it before getting on the train.

Abkürzungen *abbreviations*

DB	**Deutsche Bundesbahn**	*German railways*
IC	**InterCity Zug**	*Inter-city*
EC	**EuropaCity**	*International express*
D	**Expreß**	*express*
E	**Eilzug**	*fast train*
N	**Nahverkehr/Personenzug**	*local train*
U-Bahn	**Untergrundbahn**	*underground (railway)*

Übung 4

Complete the dialogues following the guidelines given, and then practise them.

(*a*) *You*
You want a return ticket to Köln.

Bahnbeamter	**Erste oder zweite Klasse?**
(*b*) *You*	*Second. Ask how much it is.*
Bahnbeamter	**63.50 DM.**
(*c*) *You*	*Ask when the train goes.*
Bahnbeamter	**Um halb elf.**
(*d*) *You*	*Ask where it goes from.*
Bahnbeamter	**Gleis 8.**
(*e*) *You*	*Say thank you.*

On your return journey …

(*f*) *You*	*Ask when the next train leaves for München.*
Bahnbeamtin	**Es gibt einen InterCity um 10.53 Uhr und**

	einen D-Zug um 11.18 Uhr.
(*g*) *You*	*Ask how much it costs.*
Bahnbeamtin	**Mit dem InterCity 126 DM und mit dem D-Zug 84 DM.**
(*h*) *You*	*D-Zug! Do you have to change?*
Bahnbeamtin	**Ja, in Koblenz.**
(*i*) *You*	*When do you get to München?*
Bahnbeamtin	**Um 16.44 Uhr.**
(*j*) *You*	*Where does the train leave from?*
Bahnbeamtin	**Ab Gleis 3.**

Höraufgabe 23: listen to the three customers, and for each, answer the following questions:

(*a*) Where are they going?
(*b*) What sort of ticket do they buy?
(*c*) When does the train leave?
(*d*) When does it get in?
(*e*) Do they have to change?
(*f*) How much does it cost?
(*g*) Which platform are they going from?

Whilst staying in Germany you are going to ring the station to find out details about trains. Prepare a list of questions you are going to ask in each of these two situations:
(*a*) You are going on a business trip to Hamburg with a colleague.
(*b*) Going to Rüdesheim for the day with your friend.

Am Flughafen: *at the airport*

Schlüsselwörter

das Flugzeug	the aeroplane
der Flughafen	the airport
der Flug	the flight
die Flugnummer	the flight number
der Flugsteig	gate
die Abflughalle	the departure lounge
fliegen	to fly
die Maschine	the plane
der Meldeschluß	latest checking-in time

der Fensterplatz	window seat
Wie lautet die Flugnummer?	What's the flight number?
Wann ist Meldeschluß?	What is the latest checking-in time?
Wann startet die Maschine?	When does the plane take off?
Wann landet die Maschine?	When does the plane land?
Was für eine Maschine ist es?	What type of plane is it?
Wie war die Reise?	How was the journey?
Ich bin müde.	I am tired.
hungrig.	hungry.
durstig.	thirsty.
schläfrig.	sleepy.
Es geht mir gut.	I am fine.

Übung 5

You are going to Germany. These are your flight details: Prepare what you would tell your German friend on the phone.

dep: Manchester	11.15
arr: London Heathrow	12.00
dep: London Heathrow	13.45
arr: Hamburg Fuhlsbüttel	14.15 (local time)

Flight number BA 5377

Übung 6

You have rung up to find details of your return flight. How do you ask:

(*a*) When do you leave Hamburg?
(*b*) Is it a direct flight?
(*c*) What is your flight number?
(*d*) When are you due in Manchester?

Übung 7

Complete your part in these telephone conversations with Fräulein Dellmann and Monika.

(*a*) *You*	*Hallo. How are you?*
Frl. Dellmann	**Gut danke und dir?**
(*b*) *You*	*You are fine too.*
Frl. Dellmann	**Wann kommst du nach Düsseldorf?**
(*c*) *You*	*Sunday 26th October.*
Frl. Dellmann	**Wann kommst du in Düsseldorf an?**
(*d*) *You*	*16.00.*
Frl. Dellmann	**Wie lautet die Flugnummer?**

(*e*) *You*	*LH 123. Ask where you will meet.*
Frl. Dellmann	**Ich hole dich vom Flughafen ab.** (*I'll fetch you from the airport*)
(*f*) *You*	*Say you are looking forward to it.*
Frl. Dellmann	**Bis dann. Tschüß!**
(*g*) *You*	*Tschüß! Bye!*
(*h*) *You*	*Hallo. How are you?*
Monika	**Gut danke, und dir?**
(*i*) *You*	*You are fine too. Ask when she is coming.*
Monika	**Dienstag den 4.**
(*j*) *You*	*Ask at what time she is due in.*
Monika	**Um 18.45 Uhr.**
(*k*) *You*	*Ask what the flight number is.*
Monika	**BA 345**
(*l*) *You*	*Say you will meet her at the airport.*
Monika	**Gut. Ich freue mich schon darauf.**
(*m*) *You*	*Say till then, goodbye.*
Monika	**Auf Wiederhören.**

Übung 8

How would you say you are arriving at:

(*a*) 14.30 in Düsseldorf
(*b*) 9.05 in Munich/München
(*c*) 11.30 in Cologne/Köln
(*d*) 18.35 in Hamburg
(*e*) 21.20 in Vienna/Wien
(*f*) 17.45 in Frankfurt

Höraufgabe 24: When are these six travellers arriving and what are their flight numbers?

What's in a name?

Many German placenames give you a clue about the whereabouts or origin of the place by including a word you already know. Here are a few examples:

die Brücke *the bridge*	**Innsbruck-** bridge over the river Inn
Saarbrücken	bridges over the river Saar
die Burg *the castle*:	**Freiburg, Hamburg, Augsburg** ... etc
-chen *little:*	**München** *little monks:* München was originally a small settlement of monks

der Berg *mountain:*	**Nürnberg** – Nürn mountain, Königberg – King's mountain
das Dorf *village:*	**Düsseldorf** – village on the river Düssel
die Stadt *the town:*	**Friedrichstadt** – Frederick's town
der Mund *mouth:*	**Dortmund** – mouth of the river Dort
neu *new:*	**Neustadt** – new town
der Bach *stream:*	**Marbach** – the Marbrook
der Wald *wood:*	**Mittenwald** – in the middle of the wood
das Tal *valley:*	**Wuppertal** – valley of the river Wupper
Baden *baths* (*spa*):	**Wiesbaden** – spa on the Wiese (meadow)
der Hafen *harbour:*	**Bremerhaven** – port of Bremen
die Kirche *church:*	**Oberkirch** – upperchurch
das Heim *home:*	**Rüdesheim** – Rüdi's home
der See *lake:*	**Bodensee** (lake Constance)
das Feld *field:*	**Bielefeld**

Übung 9

What do you think these names mean?

(*a*) Wolfsburg
(*b*) Fischbach
(*c*) Neuburg
(*d*) Bad Ischl
(*e*) Gelsenkirchen
(*f*) Ingolstadt
(*g*) Ammersee
(*h*) Heidelberg
(*i*) Neunkirchen
(*j*) Friedrichshafen
(*k*) Zweibrücken
(*l*) Salzburg
(*m*) Chiemsee
(*n*) Baden Baden
(*o*) Oberstdorf
(*p*) Mühlsdorf
(*q*) Steinbach
(*r*) Magdeburg
(*s*) Osnabrück
(*t*) der Schwarzwald
(*u*) Neustadt
(*v*) Rheinburg
(*w*) Guntersdorf
(*x*) Mannheim

Kulturtips

Names which we spell (or say) differently:
München *Munich*, **Wien** *Vienna*, **Köln** *Cologne*, **der Rhein** *Rhine (river)*, **die Mosel** *Moselle (river)*, **Braunschweig** *Brunswick*, **Hannover** *Hanover*, **Hameln** *Hamelin*.

15

ESSEN UND TRINKEN

Eating and drinking

In this unit you will learn

- meal times
- breakfast in a hotel
- room service
- how to buy a snack
- how to call the waiter/waitress
- how to say you need something
- how to buy ice creams and drinks

There is more about food in Unit 16.

Zimmerservice: *room service*

Schlüsselwörter

das Frühstück	breakfast
das Mittagessen	lunch
das Abendessen	evening meal
ein/en Imbiß	a snack
Kaffee und Kuchen	coffee and cakes
die Sahne	cream/evaporated milk
die Milch	milk
das Ei(er) gekocht	egg boiled
gerührt	scrambled
das Spiegelei(er)	fried egg
der Schinken	ham
der Speck	bacon
die Wurst	sausage
der Käse	cheese

die Butter	butter
der Zucker	sugar
das Brot/Brötchen	bread/breadbuns
die Konfitüre	jam
der Honig	honey
der Toast	toast
der Saft	juice
Joghurt, Cornflakes und Müsli	Yoghurt, cornflakes and muesli
was essen Sie zum Frühstück?	What do you eat for breakfast?

Übung 1

At what time ...?

(*a*) can you have breakfast?
(*b*) is lunch served?
(*c*) can you get an evening meal?
(*d*) can you get a cup of coffee?

MAHLZEITEN	
FRÜHSTÜCKSBÜFFET	6.00 h – 9.30 h
MITTAGESSEN	12.00 h – 14.00 h
ABENDESSEN	18.00 h – 22.00 h
KAFFEE IN DER KAFFEESTUBE	10.00 h – 18.00 h

Dialog

Sie	der Kellner
	Guten Morgen. Tee oder Kaffee?
Kaffee, bitte.	
	Fruchtsaft oder Cornflakes?
Orangensaft.	
	Essen Sie ein Ei?
Nein, danke.	
	Toast oder Brötchen?
Brötchen. **Haben Sie noch Milch?**	
	Bitte schön.

Breakfast in your room, fill out the breakfast order.

TRUSTEE

Park
Hotel
München

Guten Morgen!

Zimmer-Frühstücksbestellung

Zimmer Nr. | Gast | Personenzahl

Frühstück
Wann möchten Sie Ihr Frühstück – bitte kreuzen Sie die gewünschte Uhrzeit an:

☐ 7.00 Uhr	☐ 7.30 Uhr	☐ 8.00 Uhr
☐ 8.30 Uhr	☐ 9.00 Uhr	☐ 9.30 Uhr
☐ 10.00 Uhr	☐ 10.30 Uhr	

Bitte hangen Sie die ausgefüllte Frühstückskarte bereits am Abena an den Türknopf.

"Trustee Frühstück" **DM 18,—**

☐ Kaffee	☐ Tee mit Zitrone	☐ Schokolade
☐ Orangensaft	☐ Tee mit Sahne	☐ Milch kalt
☐ Grapefruitsaft	☐ Eigekocht	☐ Milch heiß
☐ Schinken	☐ Wurst	☐ Käse

Brot, Brötchen, Butter, Konfitüre, Honig

Auf Ihren Wunsch

☐ 2 Eier gebraten	☐ 2 Eier gerührt	**DM 5,—**
☐ Mit Schinken	☐ Mit Speck	**DM 7,80**

Unterschrift | Total

Die Preise enthalten Service und gesetzliche Mehrwertsteuer.
Etagenaufschlag 3,— DM.

Türknopf	door knob
Auf Ihren Wunsch	at your request (extras)

Lerntip

- Practise the dialogue, ordering different things.

Ich möchte einen Imbiß: *I'd like a snack*

Schlüsselwörter

eine Portion	a portion
Bratwurst	grilled sausage
Bockwurst	boiled sausage (Frankfurter type)
mit Pommes (frites)	with chips
mit Senf	mustard
mit Ketchup	with ketchup
mit Mayonnaise	with mayonnaise
Reibekuchen mit Apfelmus	thin potato fritters with apple purée
Waffeln mit Kirschsoße	waffles with cherry sauce
eine Dose Cola	a can of coca cola
ein Glas Limo	a glass of lemonade
eine Flasche Sprudel	a bottle of carbonated water
Wasser	water
einen Apfelsaft	apple juice
ein Bier	beer
ein Glas Wein	a glass of wine
Kleingeld	(small) change
zurück	back
und	and
Bitte schön.	Here you are.
zurück	change (lit: back)
Einmal Bratwurst mit Pommes.	Sausage and chips for one.
Zweimal Currywurst mit Pommes.	Curried sausage and chips for two.

Übung 2

How would you order these?
(*a*) chips (*b*) 2 grilled sausages
(*c*) sausage (frankfurter) and chips ×2
(*d*) can of coke (*e*) a beer (*f*) 2 waffles

Höraufgabe 25: What have these eight customers ordered?

Lerntip

- Choose a snack for yourself and two friends and work out what you would have to say to order it.

Übung 3

Ich möchte ...
Complete your part of the dialogue.

(*a*)	*You*	*You would like a sausage and chips.*
Kellner		**Ketchup oder Mayo?**
(*b*)	*You*	*Ketchup.*
Kellner		**Bitte schön. Sonst noch etwas?**
(*c*)	*You*	*Your friend wants a curry sausage and chips.*
Kellner		**Bitte schön. Und zu trinken?**
(*d*)	*You*	*You want a coke and your friend wants a beer. That's all. Ask how much it is.*
Kellner		**Das macht 22 DM.**
(*e*)	*You*	*Here you are: 50 DM.*
Kellner		**Haben Sie Kleingeld?**
(*f*)	*You*	*I have 2 DM.*
Kellner		**So, 30 zurück.**

Übung 4

Where would you expect to get the following meals or snacks? Match each one with a place.

(*a*) a quick snack
(*b*) coffee and cakes
(*c*) a pizza
(*d*) a self-service meal
(*e*) a meal and a drink (more than one place)
(*f*) an ice-cream

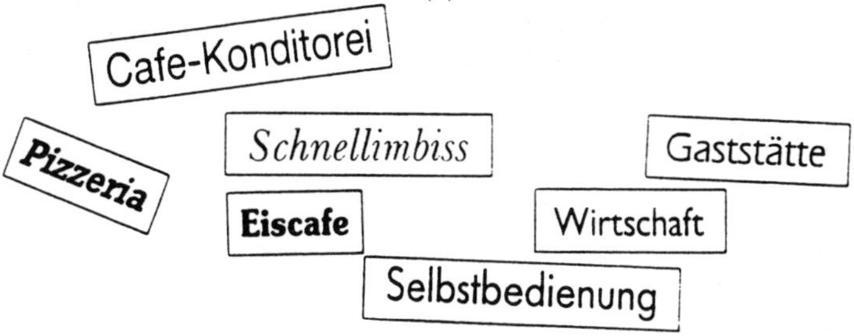

Auf dem Tisch: *at table*

Schlüsselwörter

der Teller (–)	the plate
die Tasse (n)	cup
die Untertasse (n)	saucer
die Schüssel (n)	bowl
der Becher (–)	beaker/mug
das Messer (–)	knife
die Gabel (n)	fork
der Löffel (–)	spoon
das Glas (¨er)	glass
noch	more (lit: still)/another
das Salz	salt
der Pfeffer	pepper
der Senf	mustard
das Ketchup	ketchup
die Mayonnaise	mayonnaise
die Soße	sauce

Word patterns

Ich habe	**keinen Teller**	(**der** words)
	keine Tasse	(**die** words)
	kein Messer	(**das** words)

Ich brauche	**einen Teller**	(**der**)
	eine Gabel	(**die**)
	ein Messer	(**das**)

However it won't prevent you from communicating effectively if you don't know whether a word is **der**, **die** or **das** because you can convey the meaning perfectly well without the ending. German speakers do not always pronounce them clearly themselves.

Übung 5

(*a*) How would you ask for:

(*b*) And how would you ask for more:

Kulturtips

To get the waiter's/waitress's attention, you can use:

Fräulein! — *Miss!* (calling the waitress – whatever her age.)

Herr Ober! — *Waiter!* (rather formal)

or less formally:

bitte! — *Please!*

The standard reply is:

(ich) komme gleich. — *I'm coming straight away.*

Übung 6

Complete your part of the dialogues.

(*a*) *You*	*Attract the waiter's attention.*
Kellner	**Ja?**
(*b*) *You*	*You need another plate ...*
Kellner	**Bitte schön.**
(*c*) *You*	*And the salt pot is empty ...*
Kellner	**Bitte schön.**
(*d*) *You*	*And have they got any ketchup?*
Kellner	**Sonst noch etwas?**
(*e*) *You*	*No, thanks that's all!*
(*f*) *You*	*Try to attract her attention.*
Kellnerin	**Ja, bitte schön.**
(*g*) *You*	*You need another glass.*
Kellnerin	**Bitte schön.**
(*h*) *You*	*Have they got any OK sauce?*
Kellnerin	**Es tut mir leid.**
(*i*) *You*	*You would like another beer and a glass of lemonade.*

Word building

Here are a few more examples of how German words are often combinations of shorter ones:

der Löffel *spoon*	**Eß-** *eating/dining*
Eß**löffel**	**Eß**zimmer
Tee**löffel**	**Eß**ecke
Kaffee**löffel**	**Eß**bar
Koch**löffel**	**Eß**tisch

Übung 7

Taschen- *pocket* **Küchen-** *kitchen* **Brot-** *bread*

How would you say:

(*a*) pocket knife? (*b*) kitchen knife? (*c*) bread knife?

Kulturtips

Soße as a word on its own usually means custard.
Pudding is also a sweetened vanilla sauce; it doesn't mean pudding in the sense of dessert.

In der Eisdiele: *at the ice cream parlour*

DIE EISKARTE

Venediger;	Walnuß- und Pistazieneiscreme mit Nüssen und Schlagsahne
Kopenhagener:	Walnuß, Schoko-, und Vanilleis mit warmer Schokosoße und Schlagsahne
Schwarzwälder:	Schoko-, und Vanilleis mit Kirschwasser und Sauerkirschen und Schlagsahne.
Florentiner:	Schoko-, Nuß- und Vanilleis mit Schlagobers
Kalifornien:	Pfirsisch-Eiscreme mit Pfirsichstückchen, Himbeersoße und Schlagsahne
Wiener:	Mokka- und Vanilleneiscreme mit Baiserstückchen, Schlagsahne und Schokosoße.
Italiener:	Spaghettieis mit Erdbeersoße und Kokosnusflocken

Dialog

Sie	die Kellnerin
	Was darf es sein?
Ich möchte ein Eis.	
	Hier ist die Eiskarte.
Ich möchte einmal Pfirsich Melba und einmal Bananen Split.	
	Mit Sahne?
Ja, mit Sahne.	
	Hat es geschmeckt?
Ja. Lecker!	

der Walnuß	walnut
die Nuß	nut
die Vanille	vanilla
Schoko-	chocolate
die Zitrone	lemon
der Pfirsich	peach
Himbeer-	raspberry
Erdbeer-	strawberry
die Schlagsahne	whipped cream
Mokka-	coffee
die Meringe	meringue
die Kokosflocken	coconut flakes
Welchen Geschmack?	Which flavour?
Hat es geschmeckt?	Did you like it? (lit: Has it tasted (good)?)

Lerntips

- Choose an ice cream for yourself and your friend.
- Make up an ice-cream!

Was kostet das?
What does it cost?

Biere		**Weine (¼ 1 Karaffe)**	
Löwenbräu	3,70	Mosel (bernkastel)	5,90
Export dunkel	3,60	Rhein (Liebfraumilch)	5,90
Export hell	3,60	Beaujolais	6,50
Alkoholfreies Bier	3,60	Tafelwein	4,80
Warme Getränke		**Kalte Getränke**	
Tasse Kaffee	2,50	Fanta	2,50
Tasse Kaffee coffeinfrei	2,50	Cola	2,50
Kännchen Kaffee	4,80	Tonic Water	2,60
Glas Tee		Mineralwasser	2,50
(mit Zitrone oder Milch)	2,60		
Kännchen Tee	4,80	Orangensaft	3,70
Glas Tee mit rum	6,10	Apfelsaft	2,50
Tasse Schokolade	2,40	Limo	2,30
Kännchen Schokolade	4,80	Radler	3,—

Übung 8

Was kostet das?

16

DAS RESTAURANT

The restaurant

In this unit you will learn:

- how to understand a menu
- the names of various dishes
- how to say what you like and don't like
- how to ask for recommendations
- how to say you are vegetarian

Ist hier noch frei?

Is there a place free here?

Schlüsselwörter

die Speisekarte	menu
die Weinliste	wine list
das Tagesgericht	dish of the day
die Tagessuppe	soup of the day
die Fleischgerichte	meat dishes
die Fischgerichte	fish dishes
die Vorspeisen	hors d'oeuvres
das Hauptgericht	main course
die Gemüse	vegetables
der Nachtisch	dessert
die Getränke	drinks
frisch gemacht	freshly made
hausgemacht	home-made
Was können Sie empfehlen?	What can you recommend?
Ich bin Vegetarier/in.	I am a vegetarian.
Ich esse kein Fleisch.	I don't eat meat.
Mir schmeckt es nicht.	I don't like (the taste of) it.

Es schmeckt mir gut.	I like (the taste of) it.
Schmeckt's?	Do you like it?
Hat es geschmeckt?	Did you like it?
Ja, es schmeckt sehr gut.	Yes it is very nice.
lecker	delicious
Es ist zu sauer.	It is too sour.
zu scharf.	too hot (sharp).
zu süß.	too sweet.

Lerntips

- Cover up the top part of the page and see if you can pair these up:

die Speisekarte	soup of the day
die Weinliste	dish of the day
das Tagesgericht	dessert
die Tagessuppe	main course
die Fleischgerichte	the menu
die Fischgerichte	the wine list
die Vorspeisen	meat dishes
das Hauptgericht	drinks
die Gemüse	fish dishes
der Nachtisch	hors d'oeuvres
die Getränke	vegetables

- Now cover up the German and see if you can remember it.

Dialog

Sie	der Kellner
Ist hier noch frei bitte?	
	Der Tisch in der Ecke ist frei.
Die Speisekarte bitte.	
	Bitte schön.
Was können Sie empfehlen?	
	Die Leberklöße sind frisch gemacht.
Das schmeckt mir nicht.	
	Wie wäre es mit dem Schweinefilet mit

Champignonrahmsauce und hausgemachten Nudeln?

Gut. Ich nehme es. Mein Freund ist Vegetarier.

Wie wäre es mit einer hausgemachten Gemüselasagne?

Gut. Wir nehmen einmal Matjes und einmal Aufschnittplatte als Vorspeise.

Und als Nachtisch?

Einmal Rote Grütze.

Mit Sahne?

Ja, mit Sahne und einmal Apfelstrudel.

Was trinken Sie?

Ein Glas Tafelwein.

Rot oder weiß?

Rot, und ein Glas Sprudel.

Mit Geschmack?

Nein, ohne.

Leberklöße	liver dumplings
die Champignonrahmsauce	cream of mushroom sauce
Nudeln	noodles
Gemüselasagne	vegetable lasagne
Matjes	pickled herring fillets
Aufschnittplatte	cold sliced meats (ham and salami)
die röte Grütze	a compote of red fruit (redcurrants, raspberries, etc)
der Tafelwein	table wine
mit Geschmack	flavoured (lemonade/orangeade etc)

Lerntips

- Read the dialogue and check that you understand everything.
- Read it out loud.

Die Speisekarte
The Menu

Schlüsselwörter

Fleischgerichte	meat dishes
das Rindfleisch	beef
Schweinefleisch	pork
Hammelfleisch	mutton
Hackfleisch	mincemeat
der Schaschlik	kebab
das Lammfleisch	lamb
Fischgerichte	fish dishes
der Kabeljau	cod
die Forelle	trout
der Lachs	salmon
der Hering	herring
Krabben	shrimps/prawns
das Geflügel	poultry
das Hähnchen	chicken
der Truthahn	turkey
die Gans	goose
die Ente	duck
das Omelett	omelette
das Gemüse	vegetables
Kartoffeln	potatoes
Salzkartoffeln	boiled potatoes (lit. salt potatoes)
Bratkartoffeln	roast potatoes
Pommes (frites)	chips
Erbsen	peas
Bohnen	beans
Karotten	carrots
der Spinat	spinach
der Spargel	asparagus
Bambussprossen	bamboo shoots
der Blumenkohl	cauliflower
der Kohl	cabbage
der Rotkohl	red cabbage
das Sauerkraut	sour pickled cabbage
der Salat	lettuce

Kulturtips

Wienerschnitzel (Viennese schnitzel) is a thin slice of veal or pork, which is dipped in egg before being covered with breadcrumbs and lightly fried.

Jägerschnitzel (hunter's schnitzel) is the same meat not covered in breadcrumbs, fried lightly and served with a tomato and mushroom sauce.

Zigeunerschnitzel (gypsy's schnitzel) is the same meat again without breadcrumbs, fried lightly and served with a piquant sauce with spices and green pepper.

Dialog

Sie	der Kellner
Entschuldigung. Ist hier noch frei?	
	Ja, bitte schön. Hier ist die Speisekarte.
Was für eine Tagessuppe gibt es heute?	
	Champignonrahmsuppe.
Also, einmal Tagessuppe für mich und einmal Melone.	
	Und als Hauptgericht?
Ich möchte einmal Wienerschnitzel mit Pommes und grünem Salat und einmal Schweineroulade mit Butternudeln.	
	Was trinken Sie?
Ein Glas Rotwein und ein Glas Sprudel.	
	Und als Nachtisch?
Haben Sie Obstsalat?	
	Nein, leider nicht. Aber der Apfelstrudel ist gut.
Was ist das?	
	Apfel, Rosinen und Zimt in Blätterteig.

Das sieht gut aus.
Einmal Apfelstrudel und
einmal Erdbeertorte.

Mit Sahne?

Nein danke, ohne Sahne.

Lerntips

- Read the dialogue carefully and make sure you understand everything. There are a few words that you have not met before. Can you work out what they mean?
- Read it aloud. Cover the left-hand side and answer the questions for yourself and a friend.
- Cover up the right-hand side and see if you can remember what the questions were.

Höraufgabe 26: What do these six customers order?

Gern und lieber: *liking and preferring*

Schlüsselwörter

Essen Sie gern ...?	Do you like (to eat ...)?
Trinken Sie gern ...?	Do you like (to drink ...?)
Ich esse gern ...	I like (to eat ...)
Ich esse lieber ...	I prefer (I would rather eat ...)
Ich trinke gern ...	I like (to drink ...)
Ich trinke lieber	I prefer (I would rather drink ...)
Ich mag ...	I like ...
Ich mag keine Pommes	I don't like (lit. I like no ...)
Trinken Sie gern ein Glas Wein?	Would you like a glass of wine?

Word patterns

Here are two different ways of saying you like something:

Using **gern**

Ich	**esse** **trinke** **spiele** **tanze**	gern	**Gehen** Sie gern ins Restaurant? **Essen** Sie gern Chinesisch? **Trinken** Sie gern Bier?

When you use **gern** you have to say what it is that you like doing.

Using **ich mag**

ich mag ... *I like ...*
This seems easier to use because it is more like the English:

Ich mag Bier.	*I like beer.*
but ...	
Ich mag Bier sehr gern.	*I like beer very much.*
Ich mag kein Bier.	*I don't like beer.*
and you prefer ...	
Ich mag Tee aber ich trinke lieber Kaffee.	*I like tea but I prefer (to drink) coffee.*
Ich trinke gern schwarzen Tee aber ich trinke lieber Früchtetee.	*I like (to drink) tea but I prefer (to drink) fruit/herbal tea.*

Übung 1

You want to know if your friend likes these. How would you ask?

Kulturtips

Ordinary tea is sometimes called black tea to distinguish it from the many herbal teas that are drunk in Germany.

Übung 2 *Im restaurant*

Complete your part of the dialogue, using the Schlüsselwörter or, if you prefer, the menu on page 158.

(*a*) *You* *Ask if this place is free.*
Kellner **Ja, bitte schön.**
Hier ist die Speisekarte.
(*b*) *You* *Find out what the soup of the day is today.*
Kellner **Gemüsesuppe.**
(*c*) *You* *Ask if they have tomato soup.*
Kellner **Nein, heute nicht.**
(*d*) *You* *Ask for something else.*
Kellner **Und als Hauptgericht?**
Das Schnitzel ist gut.
(*e*) *You* *No, you don't like schnitzel.*
Kellner **Essen Sie gern Fisch?**
(*f*) *You* *Choose what you would like from the menu.*
Kellner **Und als Gemüse?**
(*g*) *You* *Choose a suitable vegetable or salad.*
Kellner **Was trinken Sie?**
(*h*) *You* *Choose something to drink.*
Kellner **Und als Nachtisch.**
(*i*) *You* *Ask what they recommend.*
Kellner **Erdbeertorte.**
(*j*) *You* *Say you'll take it.*
Kellner **Mit Sahne?**
(*k*) *You* *Say yes, with cream.*
Kellner **Trinken Sie einen Kaffee?**
(*l*) *You* *Say yes, please.*

Lerntip

- Read the dialogue aloud and check that you understand all the German.

Zahlen, bitte: *the bill, please*

Schlüsselwörter

Zahlen bitte.	Bill, please (lit. pay please).
Zusammen oder getrennt?	Together or separate?
mit Bedienung	with service
ohne Bedienung	without service
MWS (Mehrwertsteuer)	VAT
Ich bin satt.	I am full.
Hat es geschmeckt?	Did you like it? (lit. has it tasted (good)?)
Das ist für Sie.	That's for you.
das Kleingeld	change (lit. small money)
das Trinkgeld	tip (lit. drink money)

Dialog

Sie	Kellnerin
Fräulein, zahlen bitte.	
	Hat es geschmeckt?
Ja, lecker.	
	Zusammen oder getrennt?
Zusammen.	
	Das macht 76.50 DM
Nehmen Sie Kreditkarten?	
	Nein. Leider nicht.
Ich habe nur einen 200 Markschein.	
	Ich habe Kleingeld.
Das ist für Sie.	
	Vielen Dank. Auf Wiedersehen.

Lerntips

- Read the dialogue and check you understand everything.
- Practise your part of the dialogue aloud.

Übung 3

These are questions you might be asked. What do they mean?

(*a*) Trinken Sie etwas dazu?
(*b*) Möchten Sie einen Nachtisch?
(*c*) Welchen Geschmack?
(*d*) Möchten Sie Ketchup?
(*e*) Hat es geschmeckt?
(*f*) Zusammen oder getrennt?

Kulturtips

The service charge is almost always included in the bill, but if you have been satisfied with the service it is normal to give an additional tip or to leave the small change, though anything under 50 Pfennig might be considered insulting.

Look at this menu and choose:

(*a*) what you will eat tonight.
(*b*) what will you eat tomorrow evening.
(*c*) what would you order for a vegetarian friend.
(*d*) what you would eat if you were very hungry and someone else was paying!

Pfefferkorn

Spezialsteaks

Rumpsteak	160 g	21,00	250 g	27,00
Filetsteak	160 g	22,50	250 g	29,00
T-Bone-Steak	500 – 600 g			29,50

Dazu reichen wir Ihnen Kräuterbutter, gebackene Kartoffel mit Kräuterquark und einen bunten Salatteller
Auf Wunsch statt Kräuterbutter Sahnemeerrettich oder rosa Pfefferbutter

Vorspeisen und kleine Gerichte

1 Matjes auf Schwarzbrot mit Zwiebelringen	3,90
Rührei mit Schinken dazu warmes knuspriges Brot	7,50
Blattspinat mit pochiertem Ei und Sc. Hollandaise überzogen	7,50
Grüne Nudeln »Milanese« (Schinken und Tomatensauce)	8,00

Rump- und Filetsteaks in verschiedenen Zubereitungen

Texanisches Steak »High Chaparral«, gegrilltes Rumpsteak mit einer feurigen Pfeffersauce, sweet-corn Schmortomate, Bratkartoffeln	22,50
Pfeffersteak »Don Juan« mit grüner Pfeffersauce und Curryreis, bunter Salatteller	25,50

Shrimps
im Blattspinatnest 9,50

Omelette mit Champignons
Sc. Hollandaise, gebackene
Kartoffel mit Butter 11,00

»Grönland«, Rührei mit Shrimps
in Butter geschwenkt, dazu
warmes knuspriges Brot 11,00

Gemischte
Fisch-Vorspeisenplatte ab 2 Personen
Avocado mit Shrimps, Lachs und
Matjes, Honig-Senf-Sauce,
Apfelsahnenmeerrettich und Preisel-
beersahne, dazu warmes knuspriges
Brot und Butter pro Person 14,50

Roastbeef mit Sc. Remoulade
und Röstkartoffeln 15,50

»Geschenkgutscheine«
Wenn Sie etwas Besonderes schenken
wollen – Geschenkgutscheine
vom Pfefferkorn

Kleine Steaks

»Südsee« drei Schweinsmedaillons
mit gebackener Banane und Ananas,
Sc. Hollandaise, Salat, dazu
warmes knuspriges Brot 16,50

»Happy day« drei Schweinsmedaillons, zwei halbe Birnen mit
grüner Pfeffersauce überzogen,
Salat, dazu warmes knuspriges
Brot 18,00

»Onkel Tom« Rumpsteak mit
tomatisierten Zwiebeln, pikant
gewürtz, Sc. Béarnaise, gemischtem
Salat; dazu warmes knuspriges
Brot 18,00

»Mignon« Filetsteak mit
Sc. Béarnaise, Champignons,
verschiedenen Salaten,
dazu warmes knuspriges Brot 21,50

Gebackene Kartoffel mit
Kräuterquark oder Butter 4,00

Bunter Salatteller 4,00

Sweet Corn mit Butter 4,00

Große Salatplatte mit Spiegelei
und Pommes frites 9,50

Salade »Niçoise« mit Thunfisch, Ei,
Oliven, dazu warmes knuspriges
Brot und Butter 12,00

Grillplatten und Filet-Spieße

Lammrücken (ohne Knochen) mit
Paprikareis und Krautsalat oder mit
Sc Béarnaise, grünen Bohnen
und Pommes frites 23.50

Drei kleine Steaks am Spieß
mit Champignons, Sc. Béarnaise,
Curryreis und Salat 22.50

Schweinefilet »Princess« mit
Spargelspitzen, Sc Hollandaise,
Kartoffel mit Butter 23.00

Goldbraun gebratene Schnitzel

Schnitzel »Weiner Art«
Bratkartoffeln und Salat 14.00

Jägerschnitzel mit Pilzrahmsauce,
grünen Bohnen und
Pommes frites 16.50

Mailänder Schnitzel
auf grünen Nudeln mit Schinken
und Tomatensauce,
Parmesan und Salat 17.00

Gerichte für zwei Personen

Zigeunerbaron, vershiedene
gegrillte Medaillons, brennend
serviert, mit verschiedenen Gemüsen,
reichlich garniert, dazu Paprikareis
und Bratkartoffeln 58.00

T-bone-Steak, am Knochen
gebraten, mit Grilltomate,
baked-potatoes und Sc. Béarnaise,
nach Wahl mit Salatplatte
oder verschiedenen Gemüsen 60.00

Desserts

Vanille-Eis mit Sahne 3.50

Schoko-Becher mit
Eierlikör ind Sahne 6.50

Nußkrokant-Becher mit
Karamelsauce 6.50

Hausgemachte rote Grütze von
Himmbeeren, Heidelbeeren, Erdbeeren
und Kirschen mit geschlagen
oder flüssiger Sahne 6.50

Vanille-Eis mit heißer Schokoladen-
sauce (Dame blanche) 6.50

Camembert gebacken, mit
Preiselbeerbirne, fritierter Petersilie,
Butter und Brot 7.00

Birne »Belle Hélène«, Vanille-Eis
mit Schokoladen-Sauce und
Sahne 7.50

Irish-Coffee mit
4 cl Irish Whiskey 8.50

17

DIE FREIZEIT

Free time

In this unit you will learn:

- how to say what you like doing in your free time
- how to ask someone what they would like to do
- about sports and hobbies
- about making arrangements
- about summer and winter activities

Schlüsselwörter

Was machen Sie gern und was machen Sie nicht gern?	What do you like and not like doing?
in meiner Freizeit	in my free time
in Ihrer Freizeit	in your free time
Schwimmen Sie gern?	Do you like swimming?
Ich schwimme gern.	I like swimming.
Lesen Sie gern?	Do you like reading?
Ich lese gern.	I like reading.
Tanzen Sie gern?	Do you like dancing?
Ich tanze gern.	I like dancing.

Using gehen with a sport or pastime

Gehen Sie gern	wandern?	*Do you like to go*	*hiking?*
	spazieren?		*for walks?*
	schwimmen?		*swimming?*
	ins Kino?		*to the cinema?*
	in ein Nachtlokal?		*to a night club?*
	joggen?		*jogging?*

Using spielen

Spielen Sie gern	Tennis?	*Do you like playing*	*tennis?*
	Karten?		*cards?*
	Snooker?		*snooker?*
	Schach?		*chess?*
	Squash?		*squash?*
	Fußball?		*football?*

Separable verbs

Ski laufen ***to ski***	**Laufen** Sie gern **Ski?**	Ich **laufe** gern **Ski.**
fernsehen *to watch TV*	**Sehen** Sie gern **fern?**	Ich **sehe** gern **fern.**
radfahren *to ride a bike*	**Fahren** Sie gern **Rad?**	Ich **fahre** gern **Rad.**

These are all verbs which split up and the prefix (first part of the word) goes to the end of the sentence.

Aussprachetip

ski sounds **shee**

Übung 1

What would you ask Fräulein Hoffmann to find out if she likes to:

(*a*) go to the cinema?
(*b*) go dancing?
(*c*) go swimming?
(*d*) play cards?
(*e*) go cycling?
(*f*) watch TV?

Dialoge
Was machen Sie gern in Ihrer Freizeit?

Sie	Herr Schwarz
Was machen wir heute Abend? Spielen Sie gern Squash?	
	Ja, sehr gern.
Gut. Wir spielen Squash. Schwimmen Sie auch gern?	

Ja. Ich schwimme gern.

Gut, wir spielen Squash und dann gehen wir schwimmen und danach gehen wir in ein Restaurant.

Gut. Ich freue mich schon darauf!

Was machen wir heute Abend?
Spielen Sie gern Tennis?

Nein. Leider nicht.
Mein Rücken tut weh.

Was machen Sie gern?

Ich gehe gern tanzen oder ins Kino.

Gut. Wir gehen zuerst ins Kino und danach in ein Nachtlokal.

dann/danach	then	**zuerst**	first

Übung 2

How would you ask Herr Schwarz's ten year old son if he likes to:

(*a*) play squash (*c*) ski (*e*) ride a bike
(*b*) play football (*d*) play tennis (*f*) play chess

Übung 3

Was machen Sie gern in Ihrer Freizeit?
How would these people answer?

(*a*)

(*b*)

(*c*)

(*d*)

(*e*)

(*f*)

Höraufgabe 27: What do these six people like and not like doing?

Haben Sie Lust mitzukommen?
Would you like to come too?

Schlüsselwörter

mitkommen	to come too (a splitting verb) (lit. to come with (me/us/you))
Ich komme mit.	I'll come too.
vorbeikommen	to come past
Ich komme ... vorbei.	I'm coming past ...
abholen	to fetch
Ich hole ... ab	I'm fetching ...
zurückkommen	to come back
Ich komme um ... zuŕuck	I'm coming back at ...
gegen	against
das Spiel	the game
danach	afterwards
vor	in front of
angeln	to fish
Ich habe Lust Tennis zu spielen.	I would like to play tennis.
haben Sie Lust Tennis zu spielen?	
Möchten Sie Tennis spielen?	Would you like to play tennis?
Nein Ich habe keinen Lust ...	No, I don't want to ...
Ich gehe lieber ...	I would rather ...
Ich bin noch nicht Ski gefahren.	I haven't skied before.
Wo/Wann treffen wir uns?	Where/When shall we meet?
Ich freue mich schon darauf.	I am looking forward to it.

heute *today*

am	heute früh/morgen
	heute vormittag
pm	heute nachmittag
evening	heute abend

morgen *tomorrow*

am	morgen früh
	morgen vormittag
pm	morgen nachmittag
evening	morgen abend

Übungen 4

Hannelore is staying with you. Tell her:
(*a*) You are going to play tennis tomorrow morning. Would she like to come?
(*b*) You are going swimming tomorrow evening. Would she like to come?
(*c*) You are going to play cards this evening. Does she want to play?
(*d*) You are going fishing this afternoon. Does she want to come?
(*e*) You are going to a night club tonight. Is she going to come?

Jürgen is staying with you.
(*f*) Tell him you are going to the local football match on Saturday afternoon.
(*g*) Ask him if he would like to come with you.
(*h*) Tell him when the match begins.
(*i*) Ask him if he would like to play tennis afterwards.

Übung 5

Complete your part of the dialogues with Hans-Peter.

Hans-Peter	Morgen nachmittag gehen wir zum Fußball, Düsseldorf gegen Bayern-München. Haben Sie Lust mitzukommen?
(*a*) *You*	*Yes, you would like to. What time?*
Hans-Peter	**Das Spiel beginnt um 14.30Uhr. Wir treffen uns um 13.00Uhr.**
(*b*) *You*	*Ask where you should meet.*
Hans-Peter	**Ich komme vorbei und hole Sie ab.**

Hans-Peter	**Morgen nachmittag gehen wir zum Fußball, Düsseldorf gegen Bayern-München. Haben Sie Lust mitzukommen?**
(*c*) *You*	*No, you don't want to. You would rather play tennis.*
Hans-Peter	**Gut. Wir spielen danach Tennis.**
(*d*) *You*	*Ask what time.*

Hans-Peter	**Um sechs.**
(*e*) *You*	*Find out where to meet.*
Hans-Peter	**Vor der Tennishalle.**

Hans-Peter	**Wir fahren morgen Ski.**
	Kommen Sie mit?
(*f*) *You*	*Yes, I'll come too but I have not skied before!*
Hans-Peter	**Kein Problem!**
	Jürgen ist Skilehrer.
(*g*) *You*	*Find out when you are going.*
Hans-Peter	**Wir fahren um 7.30 ab.**
(*h*) *You*	*And when you are due back?*
Hans-Peter	**So, um halb zehn.**
(*i*) *You*	*Good. You are looking forward to it.*
Hans-Peter	**Bis dann, tschüß.**

Im Sommer:
in summer

Schlüsselwörter

am Strand	on the beach
in den Bergen	in the mountains
auf dem Land	in the country
in der Stadt	in the town
an der Küste	on the coast
am Mittelmeer	on the Mediterranean
die Ferien	holidays
das Angebot	offer
Wo verbringen Sie Ihre Ferien?	Where do you spend your holidays?
Ich verbringe meine Ferien in den Bergen/an der Küste.	I spend my holidays in the mountains/ on the coast.

Word patterns

An, in and **auf** are trigger words which sometimes (but not always) change der, die, and das, as we've seen before.

masc.	**der** to **dem**
fem.	**die** to **der**
neut.	
plural	**die** to **den**

an + dem = am
in + dem = im

Übung 6

Can you say which 13 activities are being offered at Sonnenstrand?

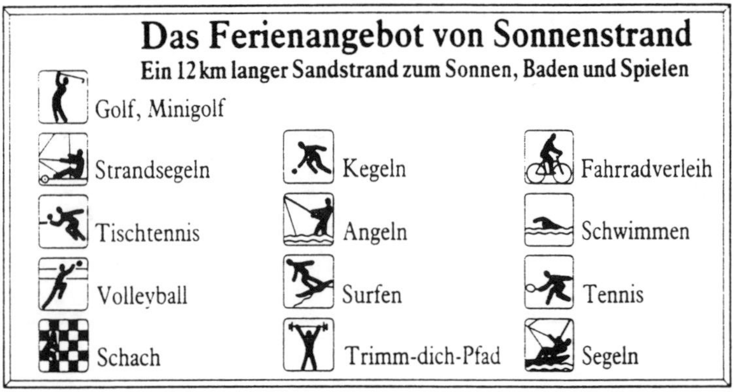
Das Ferienangebot von Sonnenstrand
Ein 12 km langer Sandstrand zum Sonnen, Baden und Spielen
Golf, Minigolf
Strandsegeln
Kegeln
Fahrradverleih
Tischtennis
Angeln
Schwimmen
Volleyball
Surfen
Tennis
Schach
Trimm-dich-Pfad
Segeln

Kegeln	bowling
Strandsegeln	beach sailing
Trimm-dich-Pfad	a fitness circuit laid out usually in a park or woodland
Fahrradverleih	bicycle hire

Dialog: Ich sonne mich: *I am sunbathing*

Sie	Hannelore
Wo verbringen Sie Ihre Ferien?	
	Im Winter verbringen wir unsere Ferien in den Alpen. Wir fahren gern Ski.
Und im Sommer?	
	An der Ostseeküste.
Was machen Sie dort?	
	Wenn das Wetter gut ist, gehen wir schwimmen und sonnen wir uns oder wir gehen surfen oder segeln.
Und wenn es schlecht ist?	
	Dann gehen wir ins Kino, oder wir machen einen Stadtbummel. Und Sie?
Wenn das Wetter schlecht ist, bleibe ich zu Hause, sehe fern oder lese ein Buch.	
	Wo verbringen Sie Ihre Ferien?
An der Küste oder in den Bergen.	
	Und was machen Sie?
Wir schwimmen und sonnen uns oder wir machen Wanderungen.	
	Was macht Herr Thomas?

Er spielt Golf oder geht angeln.

Und was machen die Kinder?

Peter spielt Tennis und fährt gern Rad und Mary verbringt den ganzen Tag am Strand.

den ganzen Tag	the whole day
Ich bleibe zu Hause.	I stay at home.

Übung 7

Was machen Sie gern, (*a*) wenn das Wetter gut ist? (*b*) wenn das Wetter schlecht ist? (tick the appropriate activities).

(*i*) Ich sonne mich.
(*ii*) Ich sehe fern.
(*iii*) Ich lese ein Buch.
(*iv*) Ich spiele Tennis.
(*v*) Ich gehe schwimmen.
(*vi*) Ich spiele Karten.
(*vii*) Ich gehe surfen.
(*viii*) Ich gehe ins Kino.
(*ix*) Ich gehe joggen.
(*x*) Ich sehe fern.

Höraufgabe 28: Was machen sie?

Im Winter: *in winter*

Schlüsselwörter

die Möglichkeiten	possibilities
Pferdeschlittenfahrten	sleigh rides (lit. horse-skate-rides)
der Schnee	snow
verschneit	snow covered
der Weg (e)	path
durch den Wald	through the wood
die Piste	piste
schön	nice
geräumt	cleared
rodeln	to sledge, toboggan
die Rodelbahn	sledge track, toboggan run
Langlauf	cross-country skiing

die Loipe	cross-country ski route
Eislaufen	skating (lit. ice running)
am See	on the lake
oder	or
auf der Eislaufbahn	on the ice-rink
Eisstockschießen	a game rather like curling
die Gondelbahn	cable railway
der Sessellift	chair lift
der Schlepplift	drag lift
der Waldweg	woodland path
entspannen	to relax
Kegeln	bowling
die Kegelbahn	bowling alley

Word building

Use these vocabulary clues and words you already know to do the exercise below:

der Schnee	*snow*
die Schlacht	*fight, battle*
die Flocke	*flake*
das Glöckchen	*little bell*
die Kette(n)	*chain(s)*
die Brille	*glasses*
die Raupe	*caterpillar*
der Sturm	*storm*
es schneit	*it is snowing*
verschneit	*snow covered*

Übung 8

How many of these new words can you make?

(*a*) snowman
(*b*) snowball
(*c*) snowball fight
(*d*) snowflake
(*e*) snowdrop
(*f*) snowchains
(*g*) snow goggles
(*h*) snow-cat
(*i*) snow storm

18

AUTOFAHREN IN DEUTSCHLAND
Motoring in Germany

In this unit you will learn about:

- buying petrol
- driving on German motorways
- using the emergency services
- what to do in case of breakdown or accident
- parking

An der Tankstelle: *at the petrol station*

Schlüsselwörter

die Tankstelle	petrol station
die Raststätte	service area
das Benzin	petrol
der Diesel	diesel
bleifrei	lead free
verbleit	leaded
der/das Liter	litre
das Wasser	water
das Öl	oil
die Luft	air
volltanken	to fill up
prüfen	to check
der Reifen (-)	tyre
der Reifendruck	tyre pressure
Selbsttanken	self-service petrol
Selbstbedienung	self-service
Münztank	coin-operated pump

Können Sie	Can you
den Reifendruck prüfen?	check the tyres?
den Ölstand prüfen?	check the oil?
die Windschutzscheibe putzen?	clean the windscreen?

Kulturtips

Most garages are now self-service, but if you buy petrol at the motorway services you will usually be served and the attendant will sometimes also wash the windscreen and expect a small tip.

There are about 4.5 litres to the gallon.

Lerntips

- Read all the words aloud.
- Cover up the English and see if you know what they all mean.
- Cover up the German and see if you can remember it.

Höraufgabe 29: What are these six customers asking?

Dialog

Sie	Tankwart
Guten Tag.	
	Guten Tag.
Volltanken, bitte.	
	Bleifrei oder verbleit?
Bleifrei.	
	Normal oder Super.
Super.	
	So, bitte schön.
Wo muß ich zahlen?	
	An der Kasse, dort drüben.
Danke schön.	

Übung 1

(*a*) What would you say to ask for these?

(*i*) 20 litres of normal/unleaded

(*ii*) 10 litres of super/leaded
(*iii*) fill up with super unleaded
(*iv*) 25 litres of diesel

(*b*) How would you ask someone to:
(*i*) check the tyre pressures?
(*ii*) clean the windscreen?
(*iii*) check the oil?

(*c*) How would you ask where you have to pay?

Übung 2

What do these signs mean? Match each sign with its meaning.

(*a*) car park (*b*) One way street (*c*) motorway exit
(*d*) petrol station (*e*) motorway services with restaurant
(*f*) way on to the motorway

(*a*)

(*b*)

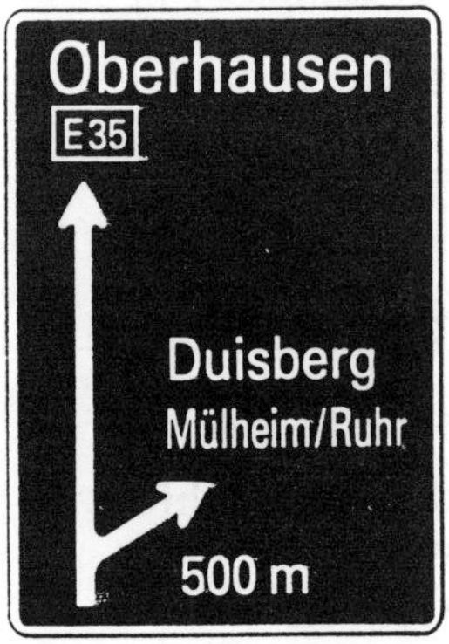

(*c*)

(*d*)

(*e*)

(*f*)

Auf der Autobahn: *on the Autobahn*

Schlüsselwörter

die Autobahn	motorway
das Autobahndreieck	motorway T-junction
das Autobahnkreuz	motorway intersection
Stau auf der Autobahn	traffic jam on the motorway
Achtung!	warning
die Raststätte	services
Richtung	direction
in der Nähe von/bei	near
zwischen	between
Wo stehen Sie?	Where are you?
Ich bin auf der A1 bei Delmenhorst Richtung Hamburg.	I'm on the A1 near Delmenhorst going towards Hamburg.

Lerntip

- Practise saying all the new words and phrases.

Übung 3

How would you tell someone you are ...?

(*a*) on the A4 between Cologne (Köln) and Aachen travelling towards Aachen.
(*b*) near Solingen travelling towards Dortmund on the A1.
(*c*) on the A5 near Offenburg travelling towards Basel.
(*d*) on the A8 near Augsburg travelling to Munich (München).
(*e*) on the B10 near Geislingen between Stuttgart and Ulm, travelling towards Ulm.

Höraufgabe 30: Where is the motorway blocked?

Kulturtips

Motorway signs are blue and white and the motorways are numbered A1, A2, etc.

The motorways which link up with international routes also have European numbers which are in green. If the two numbers are different this can be confusing. It is usually easiest to ignore the green signs and follow the blue ones.

Signs on the **Bundesstraßen** *trunk roads* are in yellow and black.

Distances are given in *kilometres* **(Kilometer)**.

To convert miles to kilometres:

divide by 5 and multiply the answer by 8
$20 \text{ miles} \div 5 = 4 \times 8 = 32 \text{ km}$

To convert kilometres to miles:

divide by 8 and multiply the answer by 5
$80 \text{ km} \div 8 = 10 \times 5 = 50 \text{ miles}$

Stau auf der Autobahn: *tailback on the motorway*

This is the sort of message you might hear on the car radio warning you about traffic problems ahead.

Durch einen Unfall ist die Autobahn bei Friedberg blockiert. Der Stau ist 11 Kilometer lang. Reisende nach München werden gebeten, die Autobahn bei Augsburg zu verlassen und die Bundesstraße 2 zu benutzen.

durch	through
bei	near, at
blockiert	blocked
Reisende	travellers
nach München	to Munich
werden gebeten	are asked
zu verlassen	to leave
die Bundesstraße	the trunk road (lit. Federal road)
zu benutzen	to use
der Unfall	the accident

Übung 4

Read the passage and see if you can answer the questions:

(*a*) Where is the motorway blocked?
(*b*) Why is it blocked?
(*c*) Where should those travelling to Munich leave the motorway?
(*d*) What road should they use instead?

Straßenschilder: *street signs*

Kulturtips

In towns there is a speed limit of 50 km/h. On other roads it is 100 km/h but there is no overall limit on the motorways although there are sometimes local restrictions.

Germans tend to drive very fast and very close on the motorways, but they are usually strict about obeying speed limits where they exist. There are a lot of radar checks and if you are caught speeding you will be expected to pay the fine on the spot.

You must use dipped headlights if visibility is poor. If you break down you must display a red warning triangle about 100 metres behind your car.

Umleitung
(diversion)

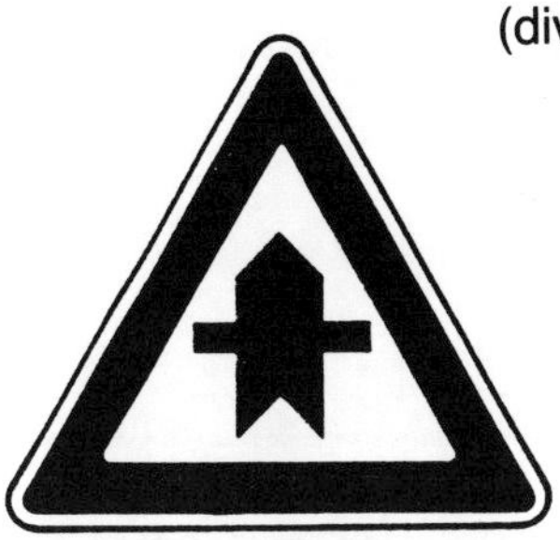

Vorfahrtstraße
(this road has the
right of way)

Baustelle
(road works)

Ich habe eine Panne gehabt: *my car has broken down*

Schlüsselwörter

Ich habe eine Panne gehabt.	I have had a breakdown.
Ich habe einen Unfall gehabt.	I have had an accident.
Was für ein Auto haben Sie?	What kind of a car have you got?
Welche Automarke haben Sie?	What make of car is it?
das Kennzeichen	car registration
Können Sie das Auto reparieren?	Can you repair the car?
Was ist los?	What is wrong?
Das Benzin ist alle.	I have run out of petrol.
Mein/e ... ist kaputt.	My ... is broken.
Sind Sie Mitglied eines Autovereins?	Are you a member of an automobile club?

Kulturtips

On the motorways there is an emergency phone every two kilometres (**Notrufsäule**) which will connect you with the nearest motorway control unit.

If you have to make a call on one you will probably be asked:

- your registration number.
- what number phone you are calling from.
- what road you are on.
- what direction you are travelling in.

Übung 5

What are you being asked?

(*a*) Was ist los?
(*b*) Was für ein Auto haben Sie?
(*c*) Wo stehen Sie?
(*d*) Welche Automarke haben Sie?
(*e*) Sind Sie Mitglied eines Automobilclubs?

Höraufgabe 31: What has happened to these six motorists?

Dialog

Sie	Autobahnhilfe
Ich habe eine Panne gehabt.	
	Wo stehen Sie?
Ich bin auf der A8 in der Nähe von Rosenheim Richtung Salzburg.	
	Bei welchem Autobahn kilometer stehen Sie?
115	
	Was für ein Auto haben Sie?
Einen Volkswagen Golf.	
	Kennzeichen?
GWY 622.	
	Was ist los?
Der Motor wird zu heiß.	
	Sind Sie Mitglied eines Autovereins?
Ja. A.A.	
	Wie ist Ihre Mitgliedsnummer?
Das weiß ich im Moment nicht. Mein Ausweis ist im Auto.	
	OK. Jemand kommt gleich.
Wann wird er hier sein?	
	In zwanzig Minuten.

Lerntips

- Make sure you understand both parts of the dialogue.
- Practise reading your part of the conversation.
- Now vary it to say:
  – you are on the A7 between Hanover and Hamburg travelling towards Hamburg, phone number 87.
  – you have a Ford Sierra, J 123 QWE,
  – you are a member of the AA (your membership number is 16 5653 3789),
  – and your windscreen is broken.

Wo kann ich hier parken?
Where can I park?

Schlüsselwörter

die Parkuhr	parking meter
der Parkplatz	car park
die Tiefgarage	underground garage (lit: deep garage)
das Parkhaus	multi-storey car park
der Parkschein	parking ticket
die Parkgebühr	parking fee
Parkverbot	parking forbidden
die Einbahnstraße	one-way street
die Ampel	traffic lights
biegen	to turn
Hier dürfen Sie nicht parken.	You can't park here.
Hier ist Parkverbot.	Parking is forbidden here.
Wie komme ich zum Parkplatz?	How do I get to the car park?
Hier dürfen Sie nicht fahren.	You can't go/drive here.
Es ist eine Einbahnstraße.	It's a one-way street.
Hier ist Anliegerfrei.	It's for residents only.
kennzeichen	registration numbers

Kulturtips

You usually have to pay fines for illegal parking, as for speeding, on the spot.

Übung 6

Who can park in these places?

Übung 7

You're about to leave your car parked in the street, when you're approached by a traffic policeman. Complete your part below.

You	Polizist
	Hier dürfen Sie nicht parken.
Ask where you can park.	
	Es gibt ein Parkhaus vor dem Bahnhof.
Ask how to get to the station.	
	Sie biegen hier gleich links ab, dann geradeaus bis zur Ampel, dann links und wieder links.
Ask where you can park.	
	Der Parkplatz ist voll. Sie müssen in der Tiefgarage einen Platz finden.
Ask where it is.	
	Gegenüber der Stadthalle.
Ask if it is expensive.	
	Eine Mark pro Stunde bis 20.00 Uhr.
And after 8.00 p.m.?	
	Nichts.
Ask if he/she has any change.	
	Was brauchen Sie?
A 50 Pf piece.	
	Nein, leider nicht. Sie müssen zum Kiosk gehen.

Kulturtips

You can tell where a German car is registered by the first letter or letters on the number plate, for example:

B	Berlin	BN	Bonn	D	Düsseldorf	DO	Dortmund
H	Hannover	M	München	MR	Marburg etc.	L	Leipzig

19

AUF DER POST
At the Post Office

In this unit you will learn:

- how to buy stamps at the post office
- how to change money at the bank
- to understand opening and closing times
- how to say you don't feel well and ask for medicine
- understanding 'the instructions on the bottle'

Auf der Post:
at the Post Office

Schlüsselwörter

die Briefmarke (n)	stamp
der Brief	letter
der Briefumschlag	envelope
das Briefpapier	letter paper
der Stift	pen
das Paket	parcel
schicken	to send
einwerfen	to post (lit: throw in)
aufgeben	to post (lit: give/hand in)
kaufen	to buy
für mich/Sie	for me/you
Wieviel kostet es?	How much does it cost
der Briefkasten	the post box
die nächste Leerung	the next collection (lit: emptying)
Ich möchte eine Briefmarke	I'd like a stamp
für einen Brief nach England.	for a letter to England.
für eine Postkarte nach Italien.	for a postcard to Italy.
zu 80 Pfennig.	I'd like a 80 pfennig stamp.

Haben Sie	**einen Stift?**
	einen Briefumschlag?
	eine Briefmarke?

Word patterns

the and *a*

der Stift – *the pen*
die Briefmarke – *the stamp*
das Paket – *the parcel*

Haben Sie **einen** Stift?
Haben sie **eine** Briefmarke?
Haben Sie **ein** Paket für mich?

Übung 1

How would you ask for these stamps?

(*a*) 1 × 1.20 DM (*b*) 2 × 1.00 DM (*c*) 3 × 80 Pf

And how would you say that you want stamps for these:

(*d*) a letter addressed
(*i*) to Italy (*ii*) to France (*iii*) to America
(*e*) postcard to England.

Dialog

You	Passant
Wo kann ich hier Briefmarken kaufen?	
	Auf der Post.
Ich möchte einen Brief einwerfen. Wo ist hier ein Briefkasten?	
	An der Ecke.
Wann ist die nächste Leerung?	
	Das weiß ich nicht.
Wo kann ich hier ein Paket aufgeben?	
	Am besten gehen Sie zur Post.

Übung 2

Fill in your part and practise these dialogues.

(*a*) *You*	*Say you want two stamps for letters to England and six stamps for postcards.*
Postbeamter	**1.00 DM. für die Briefe und 80 Pfennig für die Postkarten.**
(*b*) *You*	*Ask how much it is for a card to America.*
Postbeamter	**1.60 DM.**
(*c*) *You*	*One please.* *How much is it altogether?*
Postbeamter	**8.40 DM.**
(*d*) *You*	*Thank you.* *Say you want to write a letter and ask for writing paper.*
Frau Schulz	**Briefpapier ist in der Schublade.**
(*e*) *You*	*Ask for an envelope.*
Frau Schulz	**Auch in der Schublade.**
(*f*) *You*	*Ask where you can buy stamps.*
Frau Schulz	**Am Zeitungskiosk am Platz.**

Auf der Bank:
at the Bank

Schlüsselwörter

die Bank	bank
die Sparkasse	savings bank
etwas	some
das Geld	money
wechseln	to change
Geldwechsel	place where you can change money
der Geldautomat	automatic money dispenser
die Münze (n)	coin
der Schein (e)	note
das Kleingeld	change (lit: small money)
Welche Währung?	Which currency?
der Ausweis	identity card
der Reisescheck	traveller's cheque
der Kurs	exchange rate

unterschreiben	to sign
Ich möchte einen Reisescheck zu £100 einlösen.	I would like to cash a £100 traveller's cheque.
Ich möchte etwas Geld wechseln.	I would like to change some money.
Wie ist der Kurs heute?	What is the exchange rate today?
Wo kann man hier Geld wechseln?	Where can you change money (near) here?

Übung 3

(*a*) Ask where the *nearest* **nächste** bank is.
(*b*) Say you want to cash a (*i*) £25 traveller's cheque (*ii*) £50 traveller's cheque.
(*c*) Ask what the exchange rate is today.
(*d*) Ask where you can cash a traveller's cheque near here.
(*e*) Say you want to change some money.

Dialog

Sie	Kassiererin
Ich möchte einen Reisescheck einlösen.	
	Welche Währung?
Sterling.	
	Wieviel?
£100 **Wie ist der Kurs heute?**	
	2,79. **Haben Sie Ihren Ausweis dabei?**
Ich habe meinen Reisepaß dabei.	
	Danke. **Unterschreiben Sie hier.** **Gehen Sie zur Kasse.**

Übung 4

Fill in your part of the second dialogue, then read the whole dialogue out loud.

(*a*) *You* — *Say you want to cash a traveller's cheque.*
Kassiererin — **Welche Währung?**

(*b*) *You*	*American dollars.*
Kassiererin	**Wievel?**
(*c*) *You*	*100.*
Kassiererin	**Haben Sie einen Ausweis?**
(*d*) *You*	*Offer your passport.*
Kassiererin	**Danke.**

Übung 5

Study this rate of exchange board.

How many Deutschemarks would you get for:
(*a*) £25 (*b*) £50 (*c*) 100 Australian $ (*d*) 100 French francs

SORTEN		ANKAUF DM	VERKAUF DM
AUSTALIEN	1 $	1 24	1,36
BELGIEN	100 BF	4,69	4,87
DANEMARK	100 DKR	25,10	26,90
ENGLAND	1 £	2,88	3,03
FRANKREICH	100 FF	29,15	30,75
HOLLAND	100 HFL	87,75	89,75
ITALIEN	1000 LIT	1,34	1,42
JUGOSLAWIEN	100 DIN	0,15	0,32
KANADA	1 CAN$	1,34	1,44

Kulturtips

To change money or cash a traveller's cheque you have to go to the appropriate counter to fill in the forms and then to the cash desk to get the money, as there is usually only one person in the bank who handles the money, the **Kassierer(in).**

Some small banks are kept locked even during opening hours and you have to ring the bell to gain admittance.

Geschäftszeiten: *shopping hours*

Schlüsselwörter

Wann?	When?
Um wieviel Uhr?	At what time?
der Ruhetag	closing day (lit: rest day)
Betriebsferien	works/shop holiday
der Feierabend	end of the working day
Öffnungszeiten	opening times
offen/geöffnet	open
geschlossen	closed
um	at (time)

Banköffnungszeiten
Kassenstunden:
Montag – Mittwoch u. Freitag
8.30 – 13.00 Uhr u. 14.15 – 16.00 Uhr
Donnerstag
8.30 – 13.00 Uhr u. 14.15 – 18.00 Uhr

(*a*) When is the bank open on a Thursday?
(*b*) When is the bank open on a Monday?
(*c*) Is the bank open on a Saturday?

How would you tell your German friend:
(*a*) when the banks are open where you live?
  (*i*) Am ... ist die Bank vom ... Uhr bis ... geöffnet.
  (*ii*) Am ... ist die Bank nicht geöffnet.

(*b*) when you finish work?
Wann haben Sie Feierabend?
Um ... Uhr ist für mich Feierabend.

(*c*) which day shops are closed where you live?
Welcher Tag ist Ruhetag?
.... ist hier Ruhetag.

(*d*) what time the shops usually shut?
Die Geschäfte machen meistens um ... Uhr zu.

Kulturtips

Langer Samstag (*lit: longer Saturday*)
Shops usually shut at 1.00 or 1.30pm on Saturdays except the first Saturday in each month when they stay open until 5.30 or 6pm. In many towns there is late shopping on Thursday evenings.

Dialog

Sie	Freund
Bitte. Gibt es eine Post in der Nähe?	
	Ja, in der Hauptstraße, aber sie ist im Moment geschlossen.
Wann wird sie geöffnet?	
	Um 14.00 Uhr.
Bis wann?	
	Bis 16.30 Uhr.
Danke.	
	Bitte.

Übung 6

Put your part of this dialogue into German, then read through the whole dialogue aloud and check you understand it all.

(*a*) *You* *You want to change some money. Ask for information about the bank.*
Freund **Sie ist im Moment geschlossen.**
(*b*) *You* *Ask when it will open.*
Freund **Um 14.00 Uhr.**
(*c*) *You* *Ask when it shuts again.*
Freund **Um 16.30 Uhr.**

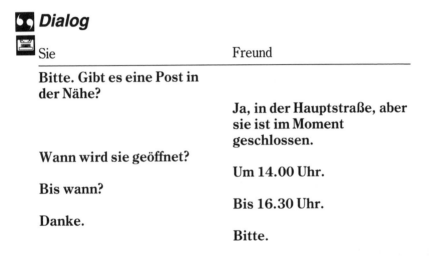

Lerntip

Revise telling the time. How do you say these times?

10.15	2.30	14.45	3.05
6.20	17.40	11.30	12.00

Übung 7

(*a*) When is this shop open?

Öffnungszeiten
Montag bis Freitag
8.45 – 18.30 Uhr
Samstag 8.45 – 13.00 Uhr
la. Samstag 8.45 – 18.00

(*b*) And when is this one not open?

Betriebsferien
14-28 Juli

Was ist mit Ihnen los?
What's the matter?

Schlüsselwörter

Ich fühle mich nicht wohl.	I don't feel well.
Ich habe ...	I have ...
Kopfschmerzen.	headache (lit: head pains).
Ohrenschmerzen.	earache.
Zahnschmerzen.	toothache.
Halsschmerzen.	sore throat.
einen Sonnenbrand.	sunburn.
eine Grippe.	flu.
eine Erkältung.	a cold.
Heuschnupfen.	hay fever.
eine Allergie.	an allergy.
Husten.	a cough.
Fieber.	a temperature.

Mein Bein tut weh	My leg hurts.
Arm.	arm
Fuß	foot
Magen	stomach
meine Hand	hand
Gesundheit!	Bless you! (lit: health)
gesund	well, healthy
krank	sick, ill
Haben Sie ein Mittel gegen ...?	Have you got something for ...?
Tabletten	tablets
schmerzstillende Tabletten	painkillers
Zäpfchen	suppositories
eine Salbe	cream, ointment
Hustentropfen	cough drops (to put in water)
Hustenbonbons	cough sweets (to suck)

Übung 8

How would you say?

(*a*) You have a cold.
(*b*) You don't feel well.
(*c*) Have you got something for sunburn?
(*d*) How often should I take them?
(*e*) You have a cough.
(*f*) You have toothache.

Höraufgabe 32: Was ist mit Ihnen los? What is wrong with these four people?

In der Apotheke: *at the chemist's*

Übung 9

(*a*) *You* — *Tell the chemist that you don't feel well.*
Apothekerin — **Was ist mit Ihnen los?**
(*b*) *You* — *Say you've got a temperature. You've got a headache and a sore throat.*
Apothekerin — **Ach, Sie haben eine Grippe. Ich gebe Ihnen Tabletten gegen Halsschmerzen.**

(*c*) *You* *Ask him if he has anything for the headache.*
Apothekerin **Gegen Fieber nimmt man am besten Aspirin.**

Übung 10

Wie oft soll ich sie einnehmen? *How often should I take them?*

See if you can match each instruction with one of the labelled medicines below.

(*a*) Every four hours with water.
(*b*) Three times a day as required.
(*c*) One tablet twice a day.
(*d*) After meals, twice a day.
(*e*) Every three hours.
(*f*) Apply/rub in as required.

(*iv*)

(*i*)

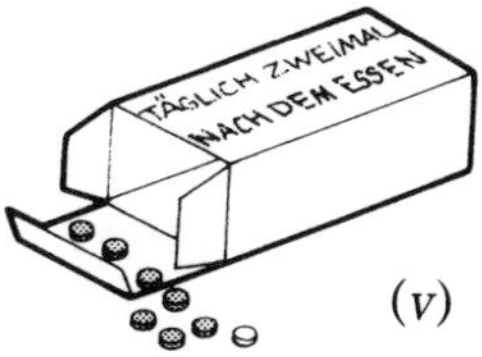

(*v*)

(*iii*)

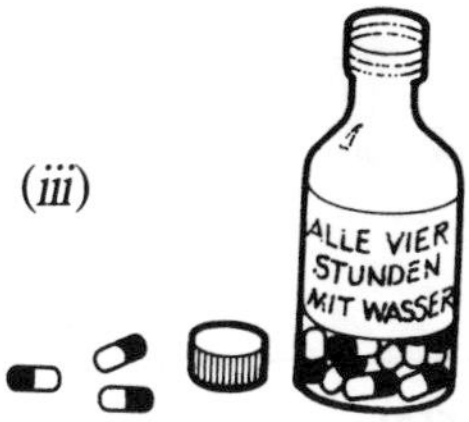

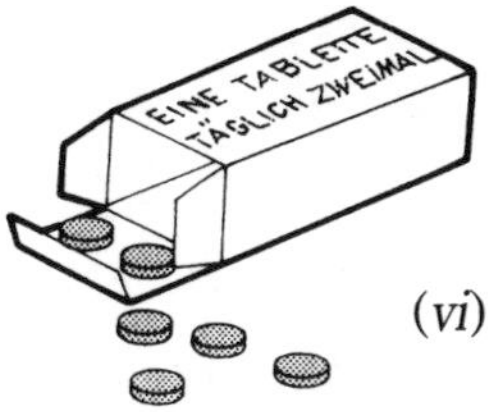

(*vi*)

(*ii*)

20

GESCHÄFTS REISE ODER BESUCH?

Business trip or visit?

In this unit you will:

- learn more about making arrangements for accommodation
- learn to read signs about the town
- revise how to ask the way to somewhere
- revise asking for things and saying if something is wrong
- learn to read the signs at a trade fair
- learn about the Länder

Haben Sie ein Zimmer frei?

Have you a room available?

Kulturtips

Übernachtung: *accommodation*
The town information bureau **Auskunftsbüro/Verkehrsamt** (or

the organisers of the trade fair or conference) can help you find accommodation.

It is possible to stay in private houses and this is usually much cheaper than in hotels.

Zimmernachweis is where you can ask about rooms available.

Schlüsselwörter

die Messe	trade fair
das Hotel	a hotel (usually international standard)
das Gasthaus / **der Gasthof**	a hotel, often typical of the region, inn
die Pension	a cheaper hotel
Vollpension	full board
Halbpension	half board
zu teuer	too dear
das Zimmer	room
Zimmer frei	rooms vacant
Zimmer belegt / **Zimmer besetzt**	rooms taken/no vacancies
Wie komme ich zum/zur ...?	How do I get to the ...?

Übung 1

Match the sign to the facilities:

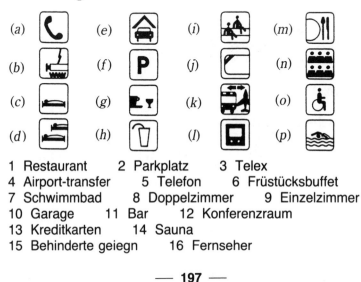

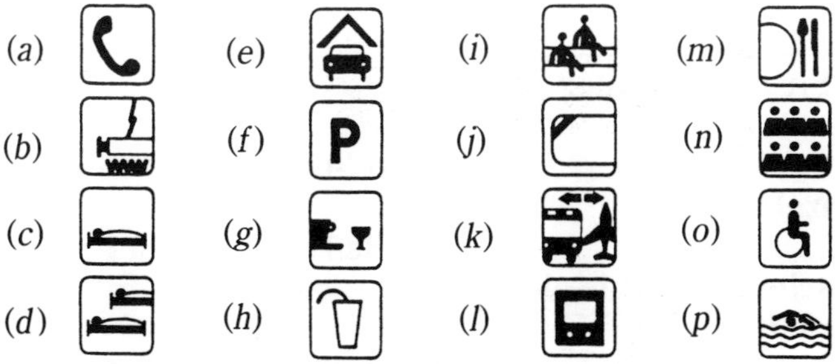

1 Restaurant 2 Parkplatz 3 Telex
4 Airport-transfer 5 Telefon 6 Früstücksbuffet
7 Schwimmbad 8 Doppelzimmer 9 Einzelzimmer
10 Garage 11 Bar 12 Konferenzraum
13 Kreditkarten 14 Sauna
15 Behinderte geiegn 16 Fernseher

Übung 2

What do these signs mean:

Zimmer frei (*a*)

Zimmer belegt (*b*)

Zimmernachweis (*c*)

Dialog

Sie

Haben Sie noch Zimmer frei?

Einzel-oder Doppel zimmer?

Ein Einzelzimmer.

Mit Bad oder Dusche?

Mit Dusche. Haben Sie ein Zimmer mit Telefon?

Ja. Im Hotel Superdeluxe. 250 DM pro Nacht.

Das ist zu teuer.

Pension Sailer.
Ein Einzelzimmer mit Bad kostet 48 DM inklusive Frühstück.

Gibt es einen Parkplatz?

Nein. Aber Sie können bis 8.00 Uhr auf der Straße parken.

Gut. Ich nehme es. Wie komme ich am besten zur Pension?

Sie fahren hier geradeaus und dann links. Die Pension Sailer ist auf der rechten Seite.

Vielen Dank. Auf Wiedersehen.

Lerntip

- Practise the dialogue, reading both parts aloud.

Ich bin zur Messe hier
I have come to the trade fair

Ankommen *Getting there*

Here are some phrases that might be useful.

Wie komme ich zur Messe?	how do I get to the fair?
mit der Straßenbahn Linie ...	tram number ...
der U-Bahn	underground
dem Bus	bus
Wo ist die Haltestelle?	where is the stop?
U-Bahnstation?	underground station?
zu Fuß	on foot
ist es weit?	is it far?
es ist gerade um die Ecke	it's straight ahead, on the corner
wie oft fährt der Bus?	how often does the bus run?
die U-Bahn?	
alle 20 Minuten	every 20 minutes
wo treffen wir uns?	where shall we meet?
wann treffen wir uns?	when shall we meet?
die Treffpunkt	the meeting place
eine Eintrittskarte	an entry ticket
ich bin Aussteller	I am an exhibitor
ich bin Einkäufer/in	I am a buyer
meine Firma heißt ...	my firm is called ...

Übung 3

Pair up the question words.

(*i*)	Wo?	(*a*)	When?
(*ii*)	Wann?	(*b*)	Which?
(*iii*)	Was?	(*c*)	How much ...?
(*iv*)	Was für ...?	(*d*)	How?
(*v*)	Wieviel ...?	(*e*)	Where?
(*vi*)	Welcher?	(*f*)	Who?
(*vii*)	Wie?	(*g*)	What kind of ...?
(*viii*)	Wer?	(*h*)	What?

Kulturtips

If you are travelling by car and want to take it to the fair every day you will find it very helpful to book parking in advance.

Remember to drive on the right and to adapt your headlights accordingly.

Übung 4

Complete your part of the dialogue, and then read the whole dialogue out loud, checking that you understand it all.

(*a*) *You* *How do I get to the fair?*
Freund **Mit dem Bus oder mit der U-Bahn.**
(*b*) *You* *Which bus?*
Freund **Linie 14.**
(*c*) *You* How often does it run?
Freund **Alle zwanzig Minuten.**
(*d*) *You* *Which U-Bahn?*
Freund **Linie 3 und Linie 5.**
(*e*) *You* *Do you have to change?*
Freund **Ja. Sie steigen am Bahnhof um.**
(*f*) *You* *How often does it run?*
Freund **Alle zehn Minuten.**
Die U-Bahn ist schneller.

(*g*) *You* *Thank you.*

You arrive, but you haven't booked your ticket in advance ...

(*h*) *You* *Say you would like an entrance ticket.*
Beamter **Einkäufer oder Aussteller.**
(*i*) *You* *You are a buyer.*
Beamter **Name und Firma?**
(*j*) *You* *Give your details.*
Beamter **Unterschreiben Sie hier.**
Das kostet 20 DM.

In der Messehalle: *at the trade fair*

Schlüsselwörter

Wo bekommt man ...	Where can you get?
einen Aschenbecher.	an ashtray.
Wasser.	water.
Blumen.	flowers.
Getränke.	drinks.
einen Imbiß.	a snack.
ein Programm.	a programme.
einen Schlüssel für Stand Nr ...	a key for stand no ...
Wo kann ich Fotokopien machen?	Where can I get photocopies?
einen Fax ab schicken?	send a fax?
Wo sind die Toiletten?	Where are the toilets?
Mein Telefon/Kühlschrank ist kaputt.	My telephone/fridge doesn't work.
Ich habe keinen Strom.	I have no electricity.
keinTelefon.	telephone.
keinWasser.	water.
Ich habe ein Telefon bestellt.	I ordered a telephone.

Übung 5

Complete your part of the dialogue.

(*a*) *You* *Say you want the key for your stand.*
Hallenmeister **Welche Nummer?**
(*b*) *You* *21.*
Hallenmeister **Bitte schön.**

(*c*) *You*	*The electricity doesn't work.*
Hallenmeister	**Ich schicke den Elektriker.**
(*d*) *You*	*Where can you get ashtrays?*
Hallenmeister	**Im Kiosk.**
(*e*) *You*	*Where can you get water?*
Hallenmeister	**Es gibt einen Wasserhahn in der Ecke.**

Höraufgabe 33: Wo?

(*a*) Where can you get photocopies?
(*b*) Where can you get a meal?
(*c*) Where can you get drinks?
(*d*) Where are the toilets?
(*e*) Where is the nearest phone?

der Eingang	entrance
der Ausgang	Exit
die Halle	exhibition hall
die Rolltreppe	escalator
der Aufzug/Fahrstuhl	lift
das Restaurant	restaurant
der Pendelbus	shuttle bus service
Erste Hilfe	first aid
der Hallenmeister	the hall caretaker

Übung 6

Which sign is which?

(*d*) NICHT RAUCHEN
(*e*) EINGANG
(*f*) IMBISS
(*b*) NOTAUSGANG
(*a*) KEIN AUSGANG
(*h*) KEIN EINTRITT
(*c*) ROLLTREPPE
(*i*) ERSTE HILFE
(*g*) AUFZUG

(*i*) entrance	(*iv*) emergency exit	(*vii*) no smoking
(*ii*) snack bar	(*v*) escalator	(*viii*) no exit
(*iii*) lift	(*vi*) no entry	(*ix*) first aid

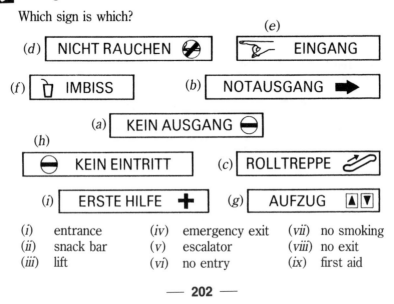

In der Stadt: *in the town*

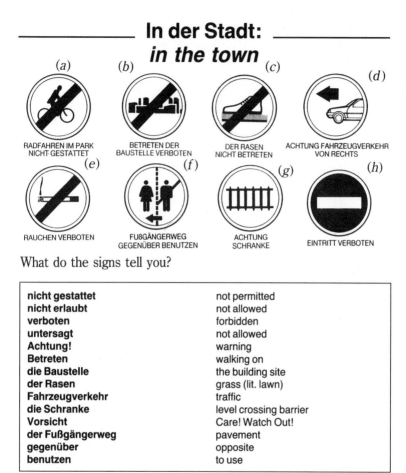

(a)
RADFAHREN IM PARK NICHT GESTATTET
(b)
BETRETEN DER BAUSTELLE VERBOTEN
(c)
DER RASEN NICHT BETRETEN
(d)
ACHTUNG FAHRZEUGVERKEHR VON RECHTS
(e)
RAUCHEN VERBOTEN
(f)
FUßGÄNGERWEG GEGENÜBER BENUTZEN
(g)
ACHTUNG SCHRANKE
(h)
EINTRITT VERBOTEN

What do the signs tell you?

nicht gestattet	not permitted
nicht erlaubt	not allowed
verboten	forbidden
untersagt	not allowed
Achtung!	warning
Betreten	walking on
die Baustelle	the building site
der Rasen	grass (lit. lawn)
Fahrzeugverkehr	traffic
die Schranke	level crossing barrier
Vorsicht	Care! Watch Out!
der Fußgängerweg	pavement
gegenüber	opposite
benutzen	to use

Übung 7 Kreuzworträtsel *Crossword puzzle*

Solve the horizontal clues and a **Land** will appear vertically.

(*a*) Ein Stadtstaat
(*b*) Die Landeshauptstadt des Saarlandes
(*c*) Dieses Land hat 4,90 Millionen Einwohner
(*d*) Die Landeshauptstadt von Niedersachsen
(*e*) Die Landeshauptstadt von Sachsen-Anhalt
(*f*) Dieses Land hat 5,50 Millionen Einwohner
(*g*) Die bayerische Landeshauptstadt
(*h*) Die Hauptstadt der Bundesrepublik Deutschland

(*i*) Die Landeshauptstadt von Thüringen
(*j*) Dieses Land hat 2,74 Millionen Einwohner
(*k*) Dieses Land hat 2,61 Millionen Einwohner

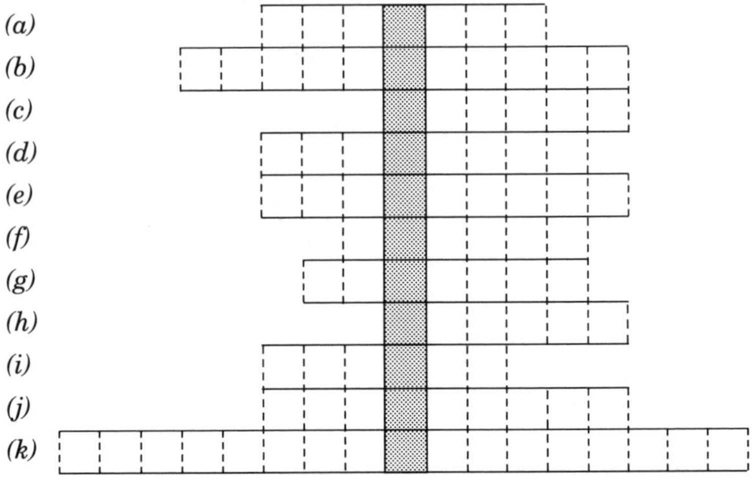

Die Länder: *the regions*

Land	*Hauptstadt*	*Einwohner (Millionen)*
Baden-Württemburg	Stuttgart	9,29
Bayern	München	10,91
Berlin	Berlin	4,25
Brandenburg	Potsdam	2,68
Bremen	Bremen	0,65
Hamburg	Hamburg	1,57
Hessen	Wiesbaden	5,50
Mecklenburg-Vorpommern	Schwerin	2,02
Niedersachsen	Hannover	7,18
Nordrhein-Westfalen	Düsseldorf	16,71
Rheinland-Pflaz	Mainz	3,63
Saarland	Saarbrücken	1,05
Sachsen	Dresden	4,90
Sachsen-Anhalt	Magdeburg	3,09
Schleswig-Holstein	Kiel	2,61
Thüringen	Erfurt	2,74

Each Land (plural Länder) has its own regional parliament (or Landtag) with much jurisdiction over regional affairs. Each Land or group of Länder has summer holidays at a different time on a rota so that not everyone is on the move at once.

Congratulations! You have completed *Teach Yourself Beginner's German* and are now a competent speaker of basic German. You should be able to handle most everyday situations on a visit to Germany and to communicate with German people sufficiently to make friends. If you would like to extend your ability so that you can develop your confidence, fluency and scope in the language, whether for social or business purposes, why not take your German a step further with *Teach Yourself German* or *Teach Yourself Business German*?

ANTWORTEN

Unit 1

1 (a) Guten Tag (b) auch (c) Herr (d) auf Wiedersehen (e) gut (f) Es geht mir gut (g) vielen Dank (h) Wie geht es Ihnen? (i) und. 2 (a) geht (b) heiße (c) mir (d) Wiedersehen.
Höraufgabe 1
(1) iia (2) iiib (3) iva (4) 1a (5) ic (6) ivc (7) iib (8) ivc
3 (a) Wie heißen Sie? (b) Ich verstehe nicht (c) Ich heiße (d) Entschuldigen Sie bitte (e) morgen (f) Herr Schulz ist nicht hier (g) Auf Wiedersehen (h) Wie bitte? (i) ein bißchen
Wiederholung
1 (a) Guten Morgen (b) Guten Tag (c) Guten Tag (d) Guten Abend 2 (c) 3 (c) 4 (i) vee gate es ee-nen (ii) unt (iii) dankuh (iv) hair (v) fr-ow (vi) ow-uch (vii) owf-veeder-say-un. 5 (a) Sie (b) bitte (c) verstehe (d) heiße, heißen (f) nicht (g) Entschuldigen (h) bißchen 6 (a) ii (b) i (c) iv (d) iii.
Höraufgabe 2
(a) iii (b) ii (c) ii (d) i

Unit 2

1 (a) Tee mit Milch (b) Kaffee (c) Kaffee mit Milch (d) Kaffee mit Sahne (e) Zitronentee mit Zucker (f) Apfelsaft (g) Orangensaft (h) Tomatensaft (i) eine Dose Fanta (j) eine Flasche Cola 2 (a) travel agents (b) traveller's cheques (c) travel costs (d) lemon tea. 3 (a) ein Glas Zitronentee (b) ein Glas Rotwein (c) Kaffee mit Sahne (d) Tee mit Milch und Zucker (e) Bier (f) ein Glas Weißwein (g) Orangensaft
Wiederholung
1 (a) Wie war die Reise? (b) Trinken Sie ... (c) Trinken Sie Kaffee mit Milch und Zucker? (d) Essen Sie ein Stück Kuchen oder ein Plätzchen? 2 (a) ii (b) v (c) iii (d) i (e) iv
Höraufgabe 3
(a) i (b) ii (c) i (d) iii.
Höraufgabe 4
(a) i (b) ii (c) iii.

Schildersprache
1 cup or pot of coffee (also decaffeinated available), mocha drink, cup or pot of ½ hot chocolate and ½ coffee, cup or jug of hot chocolate, pot of tea, pot of tea with rum, glass of camomile or peppermint tea. 2 Bringen Sie mir ein Kaffee, Tee, Bier, Cola, bitte.

Unit 3

1 eins; dreizehn; sieben; zwei; fünf; elf; acht; neun; siebzehn; sechs; vier; achtzehn; zwanzig; drei. 2 eins; zwei; drei; vier; fünf; sechs; sieben; acht; neun; zehn; elf; zwölf; dreizehn; vierzehn; fünfzehn; sechzehn; siebzehn; achtzehn; neunzehn; zwanzig. 3 (a) vier (b) sechs (c) drei (d) zwei (e) fünf (f) zwei. 4 Fünf Glas Rotwein; Drei Glas Weißwein; sechs Tassen Tee; drei Tassen Kaffee; vier Flaschen Bier; Zwei Dosen Cola
Höraufgabe 5
1–15 2–5 3–7 4–16 5–10 6–13 7–19 8–3 9–20 10–1 11–17 12–4.
5 (a) einundzwanzig (b) fünfundzwanzig (c) zweiunddreißig (d) sechsunddreißig (e) dreiundvierzig (f) siebenundvierzig (g) vierundfünfzig (h) achtundfünfzig (i) einundsechzig (j) neunundsechzig (k) zweiundsiebzig (l) fünfundsiebzig (m) vierundachtzig (n) achtundachtzig (o) zweiundneunzig (p) neunundneunzig.
Höraufgabe 6
1–32 2–36 3–54 4–21 5–88 6–92 7–25 8–72 9–69 10–43 11–84 12–47 13–58 14–99 15–75 16–61
Höraufgabe 7
(a) 24 (b) 23 (c) 52 (d) 46 (e) 83 (f) 67 (g) 93 (h) 92 (i) 84 (j) 62
Wiederholung
Höraufgabe 8
(a) 5.20 DM (b) 12.80 DM (c) 16.50 DM (d) 43.60 DM (e) 50.00 DM (f) 4.75 DM (g) 40.10 DM (h) 54.00 DM (i) 25.00 DM (j) 27.90 DM
1 (a) zwei Tassen Tee (b) drei Flaschen Bier (c) Fünf Glas Rotwein (d) Vier Stück Kuchen (e) acht Glas Weißwein.

Unit 4

1 (a) Deutschland (b) Frankreich (c) Italien (d) Polen (e) Irland (f) Großbritannien (g) Belgien (h) Spanien (i) Österreich (j) England (k) Schottland (l) Niederlande (m) Portugal (n) die Schweiz (o) Wales.
Höraufgabe 9
1 German from Stuttgart in Germany. 2 Dutch from the Hague in Holland. 3 Belgian from Brussels. 4 French from Paris. 5 Austrian from Vienna. 6 Swiss from Zurich. 7 Spanish from Madrid. 8 Italian from Milan. 9 German from Munich. 10 Scottish from Glasgow.
2 (a) Helmut (b) Waldstraße 34, Stuttgart, Germany (c) Austrian (d) single (e) 27 (f) 12 34 56 (g) Salzburg (h) 7000.
Höraufgabe 10
Name: Anna Hofmann. Wohnort: Dortmund, Neuburgring 38 Postleitzahl: 4600 Telefonnummer: 0230 22 34 56: German – married with two children, born 28/4/39 in Halle. Identity card number: 1984 2124 7D
3 (a) Haben Sie ein Zimmer frei? (b) (say your name) (c) (say where you are from) (d) (say what nationality you are) (e) (give your address) (f) (give your post code) (g) (repeat it) (h) (give your telephone number) (i) (give the dialling code) (j) (say thank you). 4 (a) Wie heißen Sie? (b) und mit Vornamen? (c) Staatsangehörigkeit/Nationalität (d) Wie ist Ihre Adresse? (e) und die Postleitzahl? (f) Wie ist Ihre Telefonnummer? (g) Wie bitte? (h) Wie ist die Vorwahl?

Unit 5

1 (a) sechs Uhr (b) Mittag/zwölf Uhr (c) Viertel nach eins (d) zehn nach zwei (e) zwanzig nach drei (f) Viertel vor fünf. 2 (a) halb sechs (b) halb acht (c) halb zehn (d) halb zwölf
Höraufgabe 11
(a) 12.30 (b) 1.30 (c) 3.30 (d) 6.30
3 (a) Wieviel Uhr ist es? (b) Wieviel Uhr ist es? (c) Vielen Dank (d) Auf Wiedersehen (e) Es tut mir leid. Ich weiß es nicht. 4 halb neun; Viertel vor neun; Viertel nach zehn; Viertel vor drei; halb sieben. 5 (a) Montag Dienstag Mittwoch Donnerstag Freitag Samstag Sonntag (b) 6.00 Uhr morgens; 9.00 Uhr früh; Mittag; 2.00 Uhre nachmittags; 4.00h nachmittags; 6.00h abends; 19.00 Uhr; Mitternacht. 6 (a) Montag um halb drei Uhr nachmittags (b) Donnerstag um elf Uhr nachts (c) Samstag um sieben Uhr abends (d) Dienstag um zehn Uhr zwanzig (e) Sonntag um Viertel vor sechs (f) Mittwoch um halb sechs (g) Freitag um Viertel vor neun (h) Dienstag Mittag (i) Donnerstag abend um Viertel nach sechs. 7 (a) Auf Wiederhören (b) Geht das? (c) Bis dann (d) Ich freue mich schon darauf.
Wiederholung
1 Es ist sieben Uhr; Viertel nach zwei; halb fünf; Viertel vor zehn; elf Uhr fünf und zwanzig; zehn nach zwölf; acht Uhr fünfunddreißig; zwanzig vor zwei; halb zehn; fünf nach sechs. 2 Vierzehn Uhr vierundzwanzig; um fünfzehn Uhr siebenundzwanzig; sechzehn Uhr zwölf; neunzehn Uhr neunundzwanzig; zwanzig Uhr einundzwanzig; zweiundzwanzig Uhr zehn; dreizehn Uhr sechsundfünfzig; dreizehn Uhr achtundvierzig. 3 (a) 4.20 (b) 2.10 (c) 9.30 (d) 10.35 (e) 3.25 (f) 6.35 (g) 8.45 (h) 2.30 (i) 3.45 (j) 8.50. 4 (a) Dienstag (b) Freitag (c) Montag (d) Samstag (e) Mittwoch (f) Sonntag (g) Donnerstag. 5 Halb elf; zwanzig nach zwei; vier Uhr; sieben Uhr; viertel vor sieben. 6 (a) I need a battery (b) I have lost my watch (c) My watch is broken. 7 (a) and (c)

Unit 6

1 (a) Nein. Das ist die Post (b) Dort drüben (c) Bitte/Nichts zu danken (d) Es tut mir leid. Ich weiß es nicht (e) Dort drüben (f) Auf Wiedersehen. 2 der Bahnhof, die Bank, die Bibliothek, die Brücke, das Cafe, der Flughafen, das Freibad, das Hotel, das Informationsbüro, die Jugendherberge, das Kino, die Kirche, die Kneipe, das Krankenhaus, der Marktplatz, der Park, die Post, das Rathaus, das Reisebüro, das Restaurant, das Schloß, der Schnellimbiß, die Straße. 3 Krankenhaus. (a) Brücke (b) Kirche (c) Theater (d) Bank (e) Marktplatz (f) Kneipe (g) Kino (h) Flughafen (i) Bahnhof (j) Rathaus (k) Post.

Höraufgabe 12
1 Nicholai church. 2 bank. 3 hotel. 4 restaurant. 5 cinema. 6 post office. 7 pub. 8 station. 9 airport 10 information office. 4 (a) Rathausplatz (b) Bahnofstraße (c) Einsteinstraße (d) Albrecht-Dürer-Allee (e) Einsteinstraße (f) Rathausplatz (g) Rosenheimer Straße (h) Waldfriedhofallee. 5 (a) in der St-Martins-Straße (b) in der Rosenheimerstraße (c) in der Albrecht-Dürer Allee (d) in der Rosenheimerstraße (e) in der Einsteinstraße (f) in der Albrecht-Dürer-Allee (g) in der Albrecht-Dürer-Allee (h) in der Albrecht-Dürer-Allee (i) Waldfriedhofallee (j) in der Bahnofstraße (k) am Rathausplatz (l) in der Bahnofstraße (m) in der Einsteinstraße (n) in der Albrecht-Dürer-Allee (o) in der Rosenheimerstraße (p) in der Bahnhofstraße.
Wiederholung
1 (a) xvii (b) xvi (c) vii (d) i (e) ii (f) ix (g) xiii (h) xix (i) iv (j) xii (k) iii (l) vi (m) viii (n) xviii (o) x (p) v (q) xi (r) xiv (s) xv.
2 Camp site; main post office; information office; police station; bus stop; motorway bridge; pedestrian area; main station; sports ground; bus station; petrol station; landing bridge.
Höraufgabe 13
(a) r (b) f (c) f (d) r (e) r (f) f (g) f (h) f (i) r (j) f
Schildersprache
i. (d) das Freibad, ii. (a) der Bahnhof, iii. (e) das Stadion, iv. (b) das Stadtzentrum, v. (f) das Rathaus, vi. (c) die Post.

Unit 7

1 (a) zum (b) zum (c) zum (d) zum (e) zum (f) zur (g) zum (h) zum (i) zur (j) zum (k) zum (l) zum. 2 (a) geradeaus, auf der rechten Seite (b) die erste Straße rechts, auf der linken Seite (c) die zweite Straße links, auf der linken Seite (d) die erste Straße links, auf der rechten Seite (e) die zweite Straße rechts, auf der rechten Seite (f) geradeaus auf der linken Seite. 3 Gibt es ... in der Nähe? (a) einen Bahnhof (b) einen Campingplatz (c) eine Post (d) einen Parkplatz (e) eine Bank (f) eine Kneipe (g) eine Bushaltestelle (h) ein Hotel. 4 (a) einzelzimmer mit Dusch; (b) Doppelzimmer mit Bad; (c) Doppelzimmer mit Dusch; (d) Einzelzimmer mit Bad. 5 (a) Bus (b) Auto (c) Bahn (d) U-bahn (e) zu Fuß. 6 (a) Gibt es ein Hotel in der Nähe? (b) Haben Sie noch Zimmer frei? (c) Wie komme ich zum Hotel ... zu Fuß; mit dem Auto; mit dem Bus? 7 (a) Sie nehmen die erste Straße rechts und X ist auf der linken Seite; (b) Sie gehen geradeaus bis die zweite Straße links und X ist auf der rechten Seite; (c) Sie gehen geradeaus und X ist auf der linken Seite nach der zweite Straße links; (d) Sie nehmen die erste Straße links und X ist auf der rechten Seite. 8 (a) toilets (b) beer garden (c) cinema (d) Rathausplatz (e) theatre (f) hospital (g) post office. 9 (a) die post (b) der Bahnhof (c) die Kirche (d) die Bank (e) das Kino (h) das Hotel (g) der Supermarkt. 10 (a) hier rechts, gleich links und immer geradeaus. (b) Ja, hier rechts, die erste Straße links, erste Straße rechts, und die Bank ist auf der rechten Seite. (c) Die Post ist gegenüber vom Restaurant. (d) Das Kino ist gegenüber der Bank. (e) Die erste Straße links und immer geradeaus. (f) Links, erste Straße rechts und erste Straße links. Das Restaurant ist gegenüber der Post. (g) hier links, rechts und dann immer geradeaus. (h) 3 Kilometer.
Wiederholung
1 (a) Wie komme ich zum Bahnhof? (b) Ist das weit? (c) Wo kann ich hier Briefmarken kaufen? (d) Wo ist hier eine Bank? (e) Gibt es ein Hotel in der Nähe? (f) Haben Sie noch Zimmer frei? 2 (a) die erste Straße rechts (b) die zweite Straße links (c) geradeaus (d) um die Ecke (e) auf der linken Seite (f) auf der rechten Seite (g) ein Einzelzimmer mit Bad (h) ein Doppelzimmer mit Dusche (i) mit dem Auto (j) zu Fuß. 3 (a) Es tut mir leid (b) Ich verstehe nicht (c) Ich weiß es nicht (d) Entschuldigen Sie, bitte (e) Wie bitte? (f) Vielen Dank
Schildersprache
(a) Post office (b) Bank (c) Town hall (d) Cinema (e) Swimming baths.

Unit 8

1 (a) i (b) iii (c) iv (d) ii. 2 (a) Spielen wir Montag Abend Tennis? (b) Gehen wir

morgen Abend ins Kino? (c) Gehen wir heute um acht Uhr in die Pizzeria (d) Gehen wir Mittwoch Nachmittag schwimmen? (e) Spielen wir Samstag um elf Uhr Squash? (f) Gehen wir Freitag Abend ins Restaurant? 3 (a) Das geht leider nicht; (b) Wie wäre es mit Donnerstag Abend? 4 (a) Gut, danke und Ihnen? (b) Am Montag, den 15. Juli. (c) Um achtzehn Uhr fünfunddreißig. (d) Um halb zehn (e) Bis Freitag Abend (f) Um Neunzehn Uhr dreißig (g) Um halb acht (h) Auf Wiederhören.
Wiederholung
1 (a) Montag den zweiten Mai um halb eins. (b) Freitag, den 24. Dezember um vierzehn Uhr dreißig (c) nächsten Sonntag um Viertel nach elf (d) nächste Woche am Donnerstag um sechzehn Uhr dreißig (e) am Mittwoch den 16. April um Viertel nach neun. (f) am Samstag den ersten September um siebzehn Uhr (g) nächsten Dienstag um dreizehn Uhr dreißig (h) am Freitag um acht Uhr.
Höraufgabe 14
1 Cafe at eleven tomorrow morning 2 Pub, tomorrow evening at 8.30. 3 15th July at 2 pm in Hamburg 4 6th April 8 pm. (other person's house) 5 24th October 7.30 pm (speaker's house) 6 7th August 7.30 pm (speaker's house) 7 16.45 Tuesday 9th Sept at the station. 8 18.35. Friday 14th March at the airport.

Unit 9

1 (a) Wie geht es Ihnen? (b) Wann kommen Sie nach London? (c) Was machen Sie morgen? (d) Spielen Sie gern Tennis? (e) Schwimmen Sie gern? (f) Trinken Sie gern eine Tasse Kaffee? 2 (a) (l) (g) (e) (m) (h) 3 (a) du (b) Wie geht es dir? (c) Trinkst du gern eine Tasse Kaffee oder ein Glas Orangensaft?
Höraufgabe 15
1 du 2 Sie 3 Sie 4 du 5 Sie 6 Sie 7 du 8 Ihnen/Sie 9 du 10 du.
Höraufgabe 16
1 Friedrich Bittner. 2 Ilse Egeberg. 3 Reinhard Drexler. 4 Wolf Kasselmann. 5 Hans Kauffeld. 6 Renate Walkemeier.
Höraufgabe 17
(i) Braunschweig (ii) Heidelberg (iii) Wuppertal-Romsdorf (iv) Iserlohn (v) Offenbach (vi) Passau (vii) Magdeburg (viii) Erfurt (ix) Cuxhafen (x) Karlsruhe (xi) Mittenwald (xii) Ingolstadt
Wiederholung
1 (a) l (b) f (c) a (d) r (e) t (f) h (g) m (h) g 2 (a) Wie heißt du? (b) Woher kommst du? (c) Trinkst du gern ein Glas Limonade? (d) Spielst du gern Tennis mit John? (e) Um vier Uhr. 3 (a) st (b) en (c) en (d) st (e) en (f) st (g) st (h) en (i) st (j) en (k) st (l) en

Quiz

1 (c) 2 (b) 3 (c) 4 (c) 5 (a) 6 (b) 7 (a) 8 (a) Munich; (b) Cologne; (c) Stuttgart; (d) Vienna. 9 (a) Rhine (b) Moselle (c) Danube (d) Die Zugspitze is the highest mountain in Germany 10 (a) 11 Baden Württemberg /Stuttgart; Bayern /München; Hessen /Wiesbaden; Niedersachsen /Hannover; Rheinland-Pfalz/ Koblenz; Nordrhein-Westfalen / Düsseldorf; Saarland / Saarbrücken Schleswig-Holstein / Kiel.

Unit 10

1 (a) e (b) en (c) st (d) wir form en. 2 (a) er (b) wir (c) sie (plural) (d) Sie polite (e) du (f) ich. 3 (a) holen (b) lernen (c) arbeiten (d) fragen (e) sagen (f) tanzen. 4 (a) gehört (b) gebraucht (c) geführt (d) gespielt (e) gehabt (f) gekocht. 5 (a) lesen (b) geben (c) schlafen (d) rufen (e) sehen (f) fahren (g) waschen.

Unit 11

1 Haben Sie ein ...? (a) Einzelzimmer mit Dusche (b) Doppelzimmer mit Bad (c) Einzelzimmer mit Bad (d) Doppelzimmer mit Dusche. 2 (a) Wo ist das Zimmer? (b) Wo ist der Fahrstuhl? (c) Wo ist das Telefon?
Höraufgabe 18
(i) double 3 nights. (ii) 1 single and 1 double 1 night. (iii) 2 doubles with bath for a week. (iv) single with shower for Monday night. (v) room with 3 beds for 1 night (25th September). (vi) double for Fri and Sat nights 12th and 13th August.

3 (a) Ich habe ein Zimmer reserviert (b) give your name (c) Nein. Einzelzimmer mit Dusche (d) Wie bitte? (e) gibt es einen Fahrstuhl? (f) Wann ist Frühstück? (g) würden sie mich um halb sieben wecken? (h) Haben Sie ein Zimmer frei? (i) Für drei Nächte (j) Doppel (k) Bad. Gibt es ein Telefon im Zimmer? (l) Was kostet das? (m) Ist Frühstück inbegriffen? (n) Ich möchte zahlen / die Rechnung bitte. (o) acht elf. Nehmen sie Kreditkarten? (p) Eine Quittung, bitte. (q) Würden Sie mich wecken? (r) Um halb sieben. (s) Zweihundert sieben. 4 (a) Entschuldigen Sie bitte (b) Mein Zimmer ist zu laut (c) Gibt es eine Dusche? (d) Ich nehme es. (e) Entschuldigen sie bitte. (f) Mein Zimmer ist zu heiß. Wie funktioniert die Heizung (g) Zimmerservice (h) Das Licht/ die Birne ist kaputt (i) Achtundvierzig. (j) Zimmerservice/ Zimmerdienst (k) würden Sie mich um halb sieben wecken? (l) dreiundsechzig. Ich möchte im Zimmer frühstücken. (m) Un sieben Uhr. 5 (a) Ich möchte nach England anrufen. (b) Ich möchte Zimmer Nummer 25 anrufen. (c) Wie mache ich ein Ortsgespräch?

Unit 12

1 (a) mein Vater (b) meine Schwester (c) meine Großmutter (d) meine Eltern (e) meine Freundin (f) meine Mutter (g) mein Bruder (h) meine Großmutter (i) meine Frau (j) mein Mann (k) mein Sohn (l) meine tochter (m) meine Oma (n) mein Opa (o) meine Schwägerin.

Höraufgabe 19
(a) Vater Oma Opa Schwester Hund (b) Vater Mutter Sohn Tochter (c) Bruder Schwester Eltern Großeltern Hund
3 (a) die Töchter (b) die Tische (c) die Stühle (d) die Häuser. 4 (a) i/ iv/ v/ vii. (b) ii/ iii/ vi. 5 (a) der Arbeitsbeginn (b) die Arbeitspause (c) das Arbeitszimmer (d) das Arbeitsende (e) der Arbeitstisch (f) die Arbeitszeit (g) die Arbeitswoche (h) der Arbeitsschluß (i) der Arbeitsvertrag. 6 (a) das Verkaufsbüro (b) das Informationsbüro (c) das Postamt (d) das Reisebüro 7 Herr Braun says (b) (c) (f) (h) (i); Silke says (a) (d) (e) (g) (j).
Höraufgabe 20
1 Car mechanic for BMW 2 Nurse 3 Business woman 4 Car electrician for a car firm 5 Hairdresser 6 Company rep 7 Business woman (in commerce) 8 Waiter

Unit 13

1 (a) Elektrogeschäft (b) Supermarkt (c) Kaufhaus (d) Konditorei (e) Bäckerei (f) Metzgerei (g) Fotogeschäft (h) Gemüseladen (i) Drogerie (j) Apotheke (k) Blumengeschäft (l) Zeitungskiosk (m) Tabakhändler. 2 (a) Film (b) CD/ Cassette (c) Briefmarken (d) Zahnpasta. 3 (a) meine Freundin (b) meinen Bruder (c) meine Großmutter (d) meine Frau (e) meinen Mann (f) meine Mutter (g) meinen Freund (h) meinen Sohn. 4 (a) Haben Sie...? (i) ein Buch (ii) Schreibpapier (iii) eine Flasche Parfüm (b) Ich suche ... (i) eine Flasche Wein (ii) Weingläser (iii) einen Bierkrug (c) Ich möchte... (i) einen Schal (ii) Ohrringe (iii) einen Kuchen
Höraufgabe 21
1 book for father 2 Winter coat for daughter 3 blue pullover for husband 4 Flowers for Frau Fischer 5 cake for Fräulein Sievers 6 toothpaste for self
5 (a) Ich möchte einen Pullover, blau, Größe 38 (b) eine Bluse, rot, Größe 34 (c) eine Hose, braun. Größe 36 (d) einen Wollschal, grün (e) ein Paar Handschuhe, schwarz (f) ein Hemd, weiß, aus Baumwolle. 6 (a) Ich möchte einen Schal für meine Mutter (b) blau (c) dunkelblau (d) Aus Wolle? (e) Wieviel? (f) Das ist zu teuer. Haben Sie etwas Billigeres? (g) Ich nehme ihn. (h) Ich möchte ein Paar Handschuhe (i) schwarz, aus leder (j) Ich weiß es nicht (k) groß (l) Ich nehme sie. Könnten Sie sie als Geschenk einpacken. (m) Haben Sie eine Straßenkarte? (n) Wo ist die Buchabteilung? (o) Wo ist der Fahrstuhl (p) Vielen Dank.
Höraufgabe 22
1 road map of North Germany 2 white shirt size 44 3 brown corduroy trousers 4 pair of jeans size 38 5 blue track suit 6 black lycra swimming costume size 40
7 (a) a shopping bag (b) a shopping list (c) a shopping trolley (d) the shopping centre. 8 (a) ground floor (b) 4th (c) 3rd (d)

4th (e) ground floor (f) 1st (g) basement (h) 3rd (i) basement (j) 2nd (k) ground floor (l) 1st.

Unit 14

1 (a) Wann kommt der Zug in München an? (b) Wann fährt der Zug ab? (c) Wie schreibt man das? (d) Wie geht es Ihnen? (e) Wo wohnen Sie? 2 (a) nach München (b) nach Italien (c) von England (d) von London. 3 (a) Nach Berlin, einmal einfach (b) Einmal nach Salzburg, hin und zurück (c) dreimal nach Mannheim, hin und zurück (d) zwei Rückfahrkarten nach Koblenz (e) Zweimal einfach nach Osnabrück (f) einmal nach Innsbruck, hin und zurück. 4 (a) Einmal nach Köln bitte, hin und zurück (b) Zweite. Wieviel kostet es? (c) Wann fährt der Zug? (d) Wo fährt er ab? (e) Vielen Dank. (f) Wann fährt der nächste Zug nach München? (g) Wieviel kostet es? (h) D Zug. Muß ich umsteigen? (i) Wann kommt er in München an? (j) Wo fährt er ab?
Höraufgabe 23
1 (a) Bremen (b) return (c) 14.49 (d) 16.12 (e) no (f) 84.50 DM (g) 8: 2 (a) Cologne (b) return (c) 9.39 (d) 13.48 (e) no (f) 216 DM (g) 10 3 (a) Vienna (b) single (c) 10.14 (d) 20.53 (e) no (f) 287 DM (g) 9
5 Ich fliege von Manchester um 11.15 Uhr ab. Ich komme in London um 12.00 Uhr an. Ich fliege ab London um 13.45 Uhr. Ich komme in Hamburg um 14.15 Uhr an Die Flugnummer ist BA 5377 6 (a) Wann ist der Flug nach Manchester? (b) Ist der Flug direkt? (c) Wie lautet die Flugnummer? (d) Wann komme ich in Manchester an? 7 (a) Hallo. Wie geht es dir? (b) Auch gut. (c) Am Sonntag den 26. Oktober. (d) Um 16 Uhr. (e) LH 123 Wo treffen wir uns? (f) Ich freue mich schon darauf. (g) Tschüß (h) Hallo Wie geht's? (i) Auch gut danke. Wann kommst du? (j) Um wieviel Uhr? Wann landet die Maschine? (k) Wie ist die Flugnummer? (l) Wir treffen uns im Flughafen (m) Bis dann. Tschüß. 8 (a) um 14.30 in Düsseldorf an (b) um 9.05 in München an (c) um 11.30 in Köln an (d) um 18.35 Uhr in Hamburg an (e) um 21.20 in Wien an (f) um 17.45 in Frankfurt an

Höraufgabe 24
1 Tues 21.35 flight LH12. 2 13.45 BA52. 3 Saturday 10.30 LH25. 4 Thurs 8.15 BA 308. 5 Fri 16th 11.05 LH 207. 6 Weds 17th 15.30 BA 125
9 (a) wolf's castle (b) fish stream (c) new castle (d) Spa Ischl (e) Gelsen churches (f) Ingol town (g) Ammer lake (h) Heather mountain (i) new churches (j) Friedrich's harbour (k) two bridges (l) salt castle (m) Chiem lake (n) Spa town (o) upper village (p) mill village (q) stony stream (r) Magda's castle (s) Osna bridge (t) the Black Forest (u) new town (v) Rhine castle (w) Gunter's village (x) Mann's home.

Unit 15

1 (a) between 6–9.30 am (b) between 12 and 2 pm (c) yes (between 6 and 10 pm) (d) yes (between 10 am and 6 pm. 2 (a) eine Portion Pommes (b) zwei Bratwürste (c) Bockwurst und Pommes zweimal (d) eine Dose Cola (e) eine Bier (f) zwei Waffeln.
Höraufgabe 25
1 Sausage and chips 2 Waffles with hot cherry sauce 3 2 Currysausage and chips 4 Frankfurter, mustard and bread bun 5 Reibekuchen (potato fritter) with apple sauce 6 Chips 7 ein Schinkenbrot und ein Käsebrot 8 2 beers and a coke.
3 (a) Ich möchte einmal Bratwurst mit Pommes (b) Ketchup (c) Ja, eine Currywurst mit Pommes (d) Eine Cola und ein bier. Das ist alles. Was macht das? (e) Bitte schön. Fünfzig mark (f) Ja, ein 2 Mark Stück. 4 (a) ii (b) i (c) iv (d) vii (e) v and vi (f) iii. 5 (a) Haben Sie ...? ein Messer; ein Glas; einen Löffel; einen Teller. (b) Salz; Ketchup; Senf; Zucker; Brot. 6 (a) Bitte! (b) Ich brauche noch einen Teller (c) Haben Sie Salz (d) Haben Sie Ketchup (e) Nein, danke das ist alles. (f) Fräulein (g) Noch ein Glas bitte (h) Haben Sie OK Sauce? (i) Noch ein Bier und ein Glas Limonade. 7 (a) Taschenmesser (b) Küchenmesser (c) Brotmesser. 8 (a) 2.60 DM (b) 4.80 DM (c) 3.60 DM (d) 2.0 DM (e) 3.70 DM (f) 2.40 DM (g) 2.50 DM (h) 6.50 DM (i) 5.90 DM (j) 3.70 DM

Unit 16

Höraufgabe 26
1 Wienerschnitzel, chips, lettuce 2 Chicken, chips and tomato salad 3 Roast pork with mashed potatoes and sour pickled cabbage 4 Trout, boiled potatoes and red cabbage 5 Pork fillet, rice and asparagus 6 Jägerschnitzel with noodles and beans
1 (a) Fleisch (b) Fisch (c) Bier (d) Tee mit Milch (e) Tee mit Zitrone (f) Kuchen. 2 (a) Ist hier frei? (b) Was ist die Tagessuppe? (c) Haben Sie Tomatensuppe? (d) Ich möchte .... (d) Nein. Das schmeckt mir nicht. (f) Ich nehme ... (g) mit ... (h) und zu trinken ... (i) Was empfehlen Sie? (j) Ich nehme das. (k) Ja, mit Sahne. (l) Ja, bitte. 3 (a) Do you want something to drink with it? (b) Do you want a dessert? (c) Which flavour? (d) Do you want ketchup? (e) Did you like it? (f) Together or separately?

Unit 17

1 (a) Gehen Sie gern ins Kino? (b) Tanzen Sie gern? (c) Gehen Sie gern schwimmen? (d) Spielen Sie gern Karten? (e) Fahren Sie gern Rad? (f) Sehen Sie gern fern? 2 (a) Spielst du gern Squash? (b) Spielst du gern Fußball? (c) Läufst du gern Ski? (d) Spielst du gern Tennis? (e) Fährst du gern Rad? (f) Sehen du gern fern? 3 (a) Ich spiele gern Tennis (b) Ich spiele gern Fußball (c) Ich fahre gern Rad (d) Ich gehe gern klettern (e) Ich spiele gern Karten (f) Ich spiele gern Golf.
Höraufgabe 27

Like	Dislike
1 swimming	dancing
2 tennis/badminton	table tennis
3 walking	jogging
4 swimming/reading	football
5 football	
6 skiing/bike	

4 (a) Morgen Vormittag spiele ich Tennis. Kommen Sie mit? (b) Morgen Abend gehen wir schwimmen. Kommen Sie mit? (c) Heute Abend spielen wir Karten. Haben sie Lust karten zu spielen? (d) Heute Nachmittag gehen wir angeln. Kommen Sie mit? (e) Heute Abend gehen wir in eine Nachtlokal. Kommen Sie mit? (f) Samstag Nachmittag gehen wir zum Fußball. (g) Kommen Sie mit? (h) Das Spiel beginnt um ... (i) Haben Sie Lust danach Tennis zu spielen? 5 (a) Ja, gerne. Um wieviel Uhr? (b) Wo treffen wir uns? (c) Nein. Ich habe keine Lust. Ich spiele lieber Tennis. (d) Um wieviel Uhr? (e) Wo treffen wir uns? (f) Gerne Ich bin noch nicht skigefahren. (g) Um wieviel Uhr? (h) Wann kommen wir zurück? (i) Gut. Ich freue mich schon darauf. 6 golf-minigolf, beachsailing, table tennis, volleyball, chess, bowling, fishing, surfing, woodland fitness circuit, cycling, swimming, tennis. 7 (a) i / iv / v / vii / ix (b) ii / iii / vi / viii / x
Höraufgabe 28
1 playing cards 2 cycling 3 watching telly 4 reading books 5 jogging 6 swimming 7 skiing 8 cinema
8 (a) Schneemann (b) Schneeball (c) Schneeballschlacht (d) Schneeflocken (e) Schneeglöckchen (f) Schneeketten (g) Schneebrille (h) Schneeraupe (i) Schneesturm

Unit 18

Höraufgabe 29
1 fill up with lead free 2 20 litres of lead free super 3 check the tyre pressures 4 20 litres leaded 5 clean the windscreen 6 Where is the cash desk?
1 (a) (i) Zwanzig Liter bleifrei, normal (ii) Zehn Liter super, verbleit (iii) Volltanken, super bleifrei (iv) fünfundzwanzig Liter Diesel (b) Können Sie ...? (i) den Reifendruck prüfen (ii) die Windschutzscheibe putzen (iii) den Olstand prüfen. 2 (a) iii (b) v (c) i (d) vi (e) ii (f) iv 3 Ich bin auf ... (a) der A4 zwischen Köln und Aachen Richtung Aachen (b) der A1 in der Nähe von Solingen Richtung Dortmund (c) der A5, in der Nähe von Offenburg Richtung Basel (d) der A8 in der Nähe von Augsburg Richtung München (e) der B10 in der Nähe von Geislingen, zwischen Stuttgart und Ulm, Richtung Ulm.
Höraufgabe 30
near Hannover, near Munich and near Berlin.
4 (a) near Friedberg (b) because of an accident (c) at Augsburg (d) the B2. 5 (a)

What is wrong? (b) What sort of car you have. (c) Where you are. (d) The make of your car. (e) If you are a member of an automobile club.
Höraufgabe 31
1 breakdown 2 broken windscreen 3 run out of petrol 4 puncture 5 no water and overheating 6 won't start.
6 (a) coaches (b) cars (c) visitors/house guests 7 (a) Wo kann ich parken? (b) Wie komme ich zum Bahnhof? (c) Wo kann ich hier parken? Der Parkplatz ist voll. (d) Wo ist die Tiefgarage? (e) Ist es teuer? (f) Und nach 8.00 Uhr? (g) Haben Sie Kleingeld? (h) ein 50 Pfennig Stück.

Unit 19

1 (a) eine Briefmarke zu eine mark zwanzig (b) zwei Briefmarken zu eine Mark (c) drei Briefmarken zu achtzig Pfennig (d) eine Briefmarke für einen Brief nach i. Italien ii. nach Frankreich iii. nach Amerika (e) für eine Postkarte nach England. 2 (a) Ich möchte zwei Briefmarken für Briefe nach England und sechs Briefmarken für Postkarten. (b) Wieviel kostet eine Briefmarke für eine Karte nach Amerika? (c) Eine bitte. Was macht das alles zusammen? (d) Vielen Dank. (e) Ich möchte einen Brief schreiben. Haben Sie Briefpapier? (f) Haben Sie einen Umschlag? (g) Wo kann ich Briefmarken kaufen? 3 (a) Wo ist die nächste Bank? (b) Ich möchte einen Reisescheck zu i. 25 Pfund ii. 50 Pfund einlösen (c) Wie ist der Kurs heute? (d) Wo kann ich hier einen Reisescheck einlösen? (e) Ich möchte etwas Geld wechseln. 4 (a) Ich möchte einen Reisescheck einlösen. (b) Dollars. (c) hundert (d) mein Reisepaß 5 (a) 75,75 DM (b) 151,5 DM (c) 136 DM (d) 3 075 DM. 6 (a) Wo ist hier eine Bank? (b) Wann ist sie offen? (c) Bis wann? 7 (a) Monday to Friday 8.45 to 18.30 and on Saturday 8.45 till 1 pm. except on the first Saturday of the month when it stays open till 6 pm. (b) Works holiday from the 14th to the 28th July 8 (a) Ich habe eine Erkältung (b) Ich fühle mich nicht wohl. (c) Haben Sie etwas gegen einen Sonnenbrand? (d) Wie oft soll ich sie einnehmen? (e) Ich habe Husten (f) Ich habe Zahnschmerzen.

Höraufgabe 32
1 headache 2 flu 3 temperature and sore throat 4 cold
9 (a) ich fühle mich nicht wohl. (b) Ich habe Fieber, Kopfschmerzen und Halsschmerzen. (c) Ich möchte etwas für Fieber und Kopfschmerzen 10 (a) iii (b) ii (c) vi (d) v (e) iv (f) i

Unit 20

1 1/m, 2/f, 3/b, 4/k, 5/a, 6/g, 7/p, 8/d, 9/c, 10/e, 11/h, 12/n, 13/j, 14/i, 15/o, 16/l. 2 vacancies; room occupied; lodgings 3 i (e), ii (a), iii (h), iv (g), v (c), vi (b), vii (d), viii (f) 4 (a) Wie komme ich am besten zur Messe? (b) Welche Bus linie? (c) Wie oft fährt sie? (d) Welche U-Bahn? (e) Muß ich umsteigen? (f) Wie oft fährt sie? (g) Vielen Dank (h) eine Eintrittskarte. (i) Einkäufer (j) ... 5 (a) Wir brauchen einen Schlüssel für den Stand (b) einundzwanzig (c) Wir haben keine Strom (d) Wo bekommt man Aschenbecher? (e) Wo bekommt man Wasser?
Höraufgabe 33
1 to the office on the 7th floor. 2 second floor 3 Snack bars everywhere, one in each exhibition hall 4 in the corner: men on left, women on right 5 in the entrance hall.
6 (a) viii (b) iv (c) v (d) vii (e) i (f) ii (g) iii (h) vi (i) ix. 7 (a) Hamburg (b) Saarbrücken (c) Sachsen (d) Hannover (e) Magdeburg (f) Hessen (g) München (h) Berlin (i) Erfurt (j) Thüringen (k) Schleswig-Holstein.

A SUMMARY OF GRAMMAR

Nouns and articles (the and a)

In German all nouns are either masculine, feminine or neuter. The words for *the* and *a* change according to the gender of the noun.

The definite article (the)

The word for *the* with	masculine words is	**der** (der Mann).
	feminine	**die** (die Frau).
	neuter	**das** (das Buch).

The indefinite article (a)

The word for *a* with	masculine words is	**ein** (ein Mann).
	feminine	**eine** (eine Frau).
	neuter	**ein** (ein Buch).

For more details see Unit 6 page 60.

Kein (*not a*)

This is a negative form of the indefinite article which we do not have in English.

Masc:	Ich habe keinen Stuhl.	*I haven't a chair.*
Fem:	Ich habe keine Zeit.	*I haven't time.*
Neut:	Ich habe kein Auto.	*I haven't a car.*

Plurals

For information about the plural forms see Unit 12 page 117.

Masculine nouns

The masculine forms **der/ein/kein** change to **den/einen/keinen** when they are used with the object of the sentence.

Der Hund	*but* Ich habe **einen** Hund (*I have a dog*)
Ein Teller	*but* Ich brauche **einen** Teller (*I need a plate*)
Kein Mantel	*but* Sie hat keinen **Mantel** (*She hasn't a coat*)

For more information see Unit 13 page 127 and Unit 15 page 150.

Nouns and trigger words (prepositions)

Some words (eg. **mit**, *with*; **zu**, *to*) act as trigger words and change **der** to **dem**, **die** to **der**, **das** to **der**, and **die** (plural) to **den**. For more information see Unit 6 pages 59–60, Unit 7 page 69 and Unit 17 page 172.

These words are always trigger words:

aus	*from/out of*	aus dem Schrank	*from the cupboard*
bei	*at/near*	bei der Post	*at the post office*
gegenüber	*opposite*	gegenüber dem Cafe	*opposite the cafe*
mit	*with*	mit dem Bus	*with/by bus*

nach	*after*	nach der Pause *after the break*
zu	*to*	zu der Bank *to the bank*

These words are usually trigger words:

an	*on*	an der Hauptstraße *on the main street*
auf	*on*	auf dem Tisch *on the table*
in	*in*	im Kaufhaus *in the store*

Personal pronouns

singular		plural	
ich	*I*	**wir**	*we*
du	*you*	**ihr**	*you*
er	*he*	**sie**	*they*
sie	*she*	**Sie**	*you* (*polite form*)
es	*it me*		

Other forms					
singular				*plural*	
mich	*me*	**mir**	*to me*	**uns**	*us/to us*
dich	*you*	**dir**	*to you*	**euch**	*you/to you*
ihn	*him*	**ihm**	*to him*	**sie**	*them* ***ihnen*** *to them*
sie	*her*	**ihr**	*to her*	**Sie**	*you* ***Ihnen*** *to you*
es	*it*	**ihm**	*to it*		

For more information about the different words for *you* see Unit 9 page 88.

Table of irregular verbs

infinitive	he/she	past (imp)	past (perf)	English
*an/rufen	ruft/an	rief/an	habe angerufen	*to ring up*
*auf/stehen	steht/auf	standauf	bin aufgestanden	*to get up*
bleiben	bleibt	blieb	bin geblieben	*to stay/remain*
essen	ißt	aß	habe gegessen	*to eat*
fahren	fährt	fuhr	bin gefahren	*to go/drive*
fliegen	fliegt	flog	bin geflogen	*to fly*
geben	gibt	gab	habe gegeben	*to give*
gehen	geht	ging	bin gegangen	*to go/walk*
haben	hat	hatte	habe gehabt	*to have*
kommen	kommt	kam	bin gekommen	*to come*
laufen	läuft	lief	bin gelaufen	*to run*
lesen	liest	las	habe gelesen	*to read*
nehmen	nimmt	nahm	habe genommen	*to take*
schlafen	schläft	schlief	habe geschlafen	*to sleep*
schreiben	schreibt	schrieb	habe geschrieben	*to write*
schwimmen	schwimmt	schwamm	bin geschwommen	*to swim*
sehen	sieht	sah	habe gesehen	*to see*
sein	ist	war	bin gewesen	*to be*
sprechen	spricht	sprach	habe gesprochen	*to speak*

tragen	trägt	trug	habe getragen	*to wear/carry*
trinken	trinkt	trank	habe getrunken	*to drink*
verlieren	verliert	verlor	habe verloren	*to lose*
wissen	weiß	wußte	habe gewußt	*to know*
ziehen	zieht	zog	habe gezogen	*to pull*
... and two regular ones				
machen	macht	machte	habe gemacht	*to make*
spielen	spielt	spielte	habe gespielt	*to play*

For more information about verbs see Unit 10, and about separable verbs see Unit 17.

ENGLISH-GERMAN VOCABULARY

* this word is sometimes a trigger word (p.215)
** this word is always a trigger word

after nach**, p.215
(this) afternoon (heute) Nachmittag, p.52
also auch
always immer
(I) am (ich) bin, p.104
and und
are sind, p.104

between zwischen*
big groß
bill, please Zahlen, bitte, p.24

Can you? Kannst du?/Können Sie?
cheap billig
child das Kind

daughter die Tochter
day der Tag
difficult/hard schwer/schwierig
to do machen

(this) evening (heute) Abend
every day jeden Tag
Excuse me Entschuldigen Sie bitte
expensive teuer

far weit
fast schnell
for für
I am looking forward to it Ich freue mich darauf
friend der Freund/die Freundin
in front of vor*

girl das Mädchen
to go (on foot) gehen; *to go (travel)* fahren
good gut

(he) has (er) hat, p.104
to have haben, p.104
(I) have (ich) habe; *Have you ...?* Haben Sie ...?; *I haven't a ...* Ich habe kein/e ...
he er
her ihr/e
him ihn
his sein/e
(in the) holidays (in den) Ferien
How? Wie?; *How many?* Wie viel?

I ich
in in*
is ist

to live wohnen

May I? Darf ich?
me mich
to meet treffen, p.51
Mr Herr
Mrs Frau
my mein/e

near neben*
new neu
nice schön
no nein

on an*/auf*
old alt
opposite gegenüber, p.72, 75

Pardon? Wie bitte?
please bitte
possible möglich

quite ganz

it's raining es regnet
room das Zimmer

she sie
short kurz
slow langsam
small klein
sometimes ab und zu/manchmal
son der Sohn
I'm sorry Es tut mir leid

thank you danke/vielen Dank
their ihr/e
there is/there are es gibt
they/them sie/sie
tired müde
to zu**
today heute
tomorrow morgen
too zu

until bis

I was ich war
woch die Woche
with mit*
without ohne
I would like ich möchte
to write schreiben

yes ja
yesterday gestern
young jung
you (see Unit 9 page 88)

GERMAN-ENGLISH VOCABULARY

* this word is sometimes a trigger word
** this is always a trigger word (**der-dem/das-dem/die-der**)

Remember:

der tells you a word is a masculine word;
die tells you a word is a feminine word;
das tells you a word is a neuter word.

der Abend *the evening*
abends *in the evening*
alt *age*
am ... (an + dem) *on the ...*, p.78
an* *on*, p.78
an/rufen *to call phone;* ich rufe ... an *I'll ring*, p.112
der Anzug *the suit*
die Anschrift *address*, p.43
auch *also*
auf* *on;* auf der rechten/linken Seite *on the right/left (side), p.68;* auf Wiedersehen *goodbye*
aus** *from/out of*
die Auskunft *information*
die Aussicht *the view*
der Ausweis *identity card*, p.43
die Autobahn *motorway*

das Bad *the bath*
der Bahnhof *the station*
bei** *at/near*, p.179
der Beruf *the job*
besetzt *engaged*
besuchen *to visit*; ich besuche *I visit*
die Bibliothek *library*, p.57
der Biergarten *beer garden*, p.62
billig *cheap*
ich bin *I am*, p.104
der Bindestrich *hyphen*, p.90
bitte *please*; Wie bitte? *pardon?*

Bitte schön *Here you are*
bleiben *to stay or remain;* ich bleibe *I stay*
brauchen *to need;* ich brauche *I need*
der Brief *the letter;* die Briefmarke *postage stamp*
die Brücke *the bridge*, p.57
der Buchstabe *the letter (of the alphabet)*
die Bushaltestelle *the bus stop*

der Campingplatz *the campsite*, p.62

da *there*
Damen *ladies*
Danke/Dankeschön *thank you*
dann *then*
das tut mir leid *I'm sorry*
der Dom *the cathedral*, p.57
Doppelbett (n.) *double bed*
Doppelzimmer (n.) *double room*, p.69
dort drüben *over there*, p.72
die Dose *tin/can*, p.148
drücken *to press/push;* ich drücke *I press*
dunkel *dark*
durch *through*
dürfen *to be allowed to*; ich darf *I may*
die Dusche *the shower*

die Einladung *the invitation*, p.79
Einzelzimmer *single room*, p.69
der Empfangstisch *the reception desk*
Entschuldigen Sie bitte *Excuse me please*
er *he*
erst/e *the first;* am ersten *on the first*
es *it;* Es geht mir gut *I am well*
essen *to eat;* ich esse *I eat*
etwas *some*

fahren *to drive*; ich fahre *I drive*
die Familie *the family*
die Feiertage *the holidays*, p.76
das Fenster *the window*
der Fernseher *the television*
die Flasche *the bottle*
der Flughafen *the airport*, p.141
die Frau *the woman/wife/Mrs*
das Fräulein *the young lady/Miss*
frei *free*
das Freibad *open air swimming pool*, p.57
ich freue mich … *I am looking forward …*
das Frühstück *breakfast*
für *for*
zu Fuß *on foot*, p.69

ganz *quite*
der Geburtstag *birthday*
gegenüber *opposite*, p.72, 75
gehen *to go;* ich gehe *I go;* Geht das? *Is that all right?;* Es geht *It's all right*
genau *exactly*
geradeaus *straight ahead*, p.68
gern/e *willingly/with pleasure*, p.160
das Geschenk *the present*
geschlossen *closed*, p.191
gestern *yesterday*
gesund *healthy*
gleich *immediately/straight away*
groß *big*
die Größe *the size*
gut *good/well*

haben *to have*, p.104; Haben Sie …? *Have you …?*
halb *half*, p.49
Haupt- *main*; Hauptbahnhof *main station*
heiß *hot*
heißen *to be called;* ich heiße *I am called*
der Herr *the man/Mr/husband;* die Herren *men*
heute *today*, p.169
hier *here*
holen *to fetch;* ich hole *I fetch*, p.98

ich *I*
immer *always*
inbegriffen *included*

ja *yes;* jawohl *yes indeed*
die Jugendherberge *the youth hostel*

kalt *cold*
kaputt *broken*
kaufen *to buy;* ich kaufe *I buy*
kein/e *not a*
Ich habe kein/e … *I haven't a …*
der Kellner *the waiter*
das Kino *the cinema*, p.57
die Kirche *the church*, p.57
klein *small*
die Kneipe *the pub*, p.57
kommen *to come;* ich komme *I come*
Kopfschmerzen (pl.) *headache*, p.193
krank *ill*, p.193
das Krankenhaus *the hospital*, p.57

langsam *slow;* langsamer *slower*
laut *loud/noisy*
ledig *unmarried*, p.43
leider *unfortunately*
lieber *rather;* ich trinke lieber Tee *I would prefer tea*
links *left*

machen *to make;* ich mache *I make*, p.96
der Mann *the husband*
die Milch *milk*
mit** *with*, p.75
ich möchte *I would like*, p.113
morgen *tomorrow*, p.169
müde *tired*

nach** *after/past*, p.48
nächst/e *next*, p.81
die Nacht *the night*
nehmen *to take;* ich nehme *I take*, p.68
nicht *not*
noch *still/yet/more*
nur *only*

oder *or*
ohne *without*
Ostern *Easter*, p.76

die Polizei *the police*
die Postleitzahl *the post code*, p.38
prima! *great!*, p.81

die Quittung *a receipt*

das Rathaus *the town hall*, p.57
rechts *right*
die Reise *the journey*
rot *red*

das Schloß *the castle*
der Schlüssel *the key*
schnell *quick/fast*
schwimmen *to swim;* ich schwimme *I swim*
sehen *to see;* ich sehe *I see*
sehr *very*
seit** *since*
sie *she/they;* Sie *you*, p.88
sind *are;* sein, p.104 *to be* Sind Sie ...? *Are you ...?*
spielen *to play;* ich spiele *I play*
sprechen *to speak;* ich spreche *I speak*

die Straße *the street*, p.29
das Stück *the piece*
süß *sweet*

die Tankstelle *petrol station*, p.176
teuer *expensive*
treffen *to meet;* Treffen wir uns? *Shall we meet?*, p.51
trinken *to drink;* ich trinke *I drink*
trocken *dry*
Tschüs/Tschüß *'bye*

die Uhr *the clock*, p.49
um *at/around*, p.191

verboten *forbidden*
verheiratet *married*
verlieren *to lose;* verloren *lost*
verstehen *to understand;* ich verstehe *I understand*
viel/e *many;* vielen Dank *many thanks*
viertel *quarter*, p.48
von** *of/from*
vor* *before/to*, p.48
die Vorwahl *the telephone code*, p.38

wählen *to dial/to choose*, p.38
Wann? *When?*
Was? *What?;* Was für ...? *What kind of ...?*
der Wecker *alarm clock*, p.55
weiß *white*
ich weiß *I know*
Weihnachten *Christmas*
weit *far*
Welche/r? *Which?*
Wer? *Who?*
Wie? *How?;* Wie bitte? *Pardon?;* Wie viele? *How many?*
Wo? *Where?*
die Woche *the week*, p.51
wohnen *to live;* ich wohne *I live*

zahlen *to pay;* Zahlen bitte! *Bill please!*, p.24
die Zeit *the time*
ziemlich *rather*
das Zimmer *the room*
zu** *to;* zu *too*, p.66
Zucker *sugar*
zuerst *at first*
der Zug *the train;* mit dem Zug *by train*
zwischen *between*, p.179